CORNELL SCIENTIFIC INQUIRY SERIES
STUDENT EDITION

Assessing
Toxic Risk

Shirley Watt Ireton, Director
Judy Cusick, Associate Editor
Carol Duval, Associate Editor
Linda Olliver, Cover Design

Art and Design
Linda Olliver, Director
NSTA Web
Tim Weber, Webmaster
Periodicals Publishing
Shelley Carey, Director
Printing and Production
Catherine Lorrain-Hale, Director
Publications Operations
Erin Miller, Manager
*sci*LINKS
Tyson Brown, Manager

National Science Teachers Association
Gerald F. Wheeler, Executive Director
David Beacom, Publisher

NSTA Press, NSTA Journals,
and the NSTA Web site deliver
high-quality resources for
science educators.

Cover Image from Tony Stone©.

Assessing Toxic Risk
NSTA Stock Number: PB162X1S
ISBN: 0-87355-222-9
Library of Congress Control Number: 2001093728

*Featuring sciLINKS®—a way to connect text and the Internet. Up-to-the-
minute online content, classroom ideas, and other materials are just a click
away. Go to page ix to learn more about this new educational resource.*

This material is based on work supported by the National Science Foundation under Grant No. 96-18142.
Any opinions, findings, conclusions, or recommendations expressed in this material are those of the authors
and do not necessarily reflect the views of the National Science Foundation.

CORNELL SCIENTIFIC INQUIRY SERIES

STUDENT EDITION

Assessing Toxic Risk

BY THE ENVIRONMENTAL INQUIRY LEADERSHIP TEAM:

NANCY M. TRAUTMANN
WILLIAM S. CARLSEN
MARIANNE E. KRASNY, AND
CHRISTINE M. CUNNINGHAM

WITH PATRICIA CARROLL (NEWARK VALLEY HIGH SCHOOL)
AND JANINE GUADAGNO (TABERNACLE CHRISTIAN ACADEMY)
AND CORNELL SCIENTIST STEPHEN M. PENNINGROTH

National Science Teachers Association

Table of Contents

STUDENT EDITION

PREFACE

WHY STUDY TOXIC RISK?

News reports frequently include stories about toxic chemicals in our food, water, and environment. Have you ever wondered how to decide which of these are worth worrying about? We all make decisions about questions such as "Is it safe to drink diet soda?" We also decide about broader political issues such as "What concentration of arsenic should be allowed in public drinking water supplies?"

Too often decisions such as these are based on misconceptions about what is "safe" and what involves too great a risk. Through learning some of the basic concepts of toxicology, you will become better prepared to make reasoned decisions about issues such as these.

CARRYING OUT YOUR OWN RESEARCH

This book is part of the Environmental Inquiry series developed at Cornell University to enable you to conduct scientific research on relevant environmental topics. Using the research protocols in this book, you will learn to carry out experiments called bioassays. These are ways of evaluating the toxicity of a substance by measuring its effect on living things. Professional scientists use these same research techniques to evaluate the toxicity of chemical solutions and environmental samples.

We hope that your research experiences will help you to ask your own questions and to think critically when you hear toxicology stories in the news. What does it mean to say that something is "toxic"? Or to say that we want our food and water to be "safe"? Many people believe that scientists hold the answers to questions such as these. In fact, you will see that science provides only part of the answer, and human judgment provides the other critical piece. As you do your experiments, you may find yourself coming up with new questions and uncertainties rather than with concrete answers. Don't worry—that is the way science works! One of the things that makes science exciting is that it is a continuous process of discovery, and there is always more to be learned.

HOW TO USE THIS BOOK

This book is designed to help you experience some of the ways in which scientists work together to discuss ideas, exchange feedback, and collaborate on joint projects.

First, you will find five chapters with background information about chemical toxicity and risk. With the understanding you gain from these chapters, you are likely to find yourself asking lots of questions about chemicals in your home, school, and environment. The next section is made up of seven research protocols—these are instructions for procedures you can use to begin addressing questions about chemical toxicity. Finally, there is a discussion of ideas for research projects you could conduct using the bioassay protocols you have learned. At the back of the book is a collection of worksheets that will guide your progress through the various steps of designing and carrying out an experiment, presenting your results, and exchanging feedback with fellow students.

As you make your way through your toxicology research, we encourage you to visit our website *http://ei.cornell.edu* to share your experiences, observations, and questions with other participating students. Have fun, and good luck with your research!

—Nancy Trautmann
Lead Author

How can you avoid searching hundreds of science Web sites to locate the best sources of information on a given topic? SciLinks, created and maintained by the National Science Teachers Association (NSTA), has the answer.

In a SciLinked text, such as this one, you'll find a logo and keyword near a concept your class is studying, a URL (*www.scilinks.org*), and a keyword code. Simply go to the SciLinks Web site, type in the code, and receive an annotated listing of as many as 15 Web pages—all of which have gone through an extensive review process conducted by a team of science educators. SciLinks is your best source of pertinent, trustworthy Internet links on subjects from astronomy to zoology.

Need more information? Take a tour—*www.scilinks.org/tour*

UNDERSTANDING TOXIC RISK

CHAPTER 1

THE DOSE MAKES THE POISON

Which would you prefer to drink—a cup of caffeine or a cup of trichloroethylene? Chances are good that your response was "caffeine." Caffeine occurs naturally in coffee, tea, and chocolate, and it is added to sodas and other types of drinks and foods. Trichloroethylene, on the other hand, is a solvent used to dissolve grease, and it is also a common ingredient in glues, paint removers, and cleaning fluids. Trichloroethylene does not occur naturally in the environment, but it is sometimes found as a pollutant in groundwater and surface water.

So, which would be better to drink? Believe it or not, caffeine is more poisonous than trichloroethylene. At low concentrations, caffeine is used as a food additive because of its effects as a stimulant—it helps people to stay awake and to feel lively. However, at concentrations higher than those found in food products, caffeine can cause insomnia, dizziness, headaches, vomiting, and heart problems. In studies of laboratory animals, high doses of caffeine have caused birth defects and cancer.

Does this mean you should think twice about reaching for that cup of cocoa or tea? No, there's more to the story than that. What it does mean is that many common substances found in food and drinks are *toxic*, or poisonous, if you eat or drink large enough quantities. The amount of caffeine in a normal human diet does not cause illness, but just 50 times this amount is enough to be fatal.

Trichloroethylene is less toxic over the short term than caffeine, but it is not harmless. In fact, long-term exposure may cause a variety of health problems, including cancer as well as damage to liver and kidneys.

Toxicity indicates how poisonous a substance is to biological organisms.

ANY CHEMICAL CAN BE TOXIC

Any chemical can be toxic if you eat, drink, or absorb too much of it. Even water can kill you if you drink too much too quickly! Back in the early 1500s, a Swiss doctor named Philippus Aureolus Theophrastus Bombastus von Hohenheim-Paracelsus wrote:

> All substances are poisons; there is none which is not a poison. The right dose differentiates a poison from a remedy.

Topic: trichloroethylene
Go to: www.sciLINKS.org
Code: ATR01

Any chemical can be toxic if you eat, drink, or absorb too much of it.

Paracelsus was one of the first people to recognize that a chemical can be harmless or even beneficial at low concentrations but poisonous at higher ones. That is why it is so important to take medicine in the correct dosage. Even vitamin pills can kill you if you swallow too many in too short a period of time. For example, vitamin D is an important nutrient, but it also is a highly toxic chemical. In tiny amounts it is good for you, but taking more than the recommended dose can cause serious health problems, including kidney stones, high blood pressure, deafness, and even death.

ARE NATURAL CHEMICALS SAFER?

Synthetic chemicals are made by people rather than nature. They are composed of natural elements such as carbon, hydrogen, nitrogen, and chlorine. We manufacture synthetic compounds to use in a wide variety of products such as cleaners, deodorants, food additives, and pesticides.

Toxins are toxic chemicals created by plants and animals, usually for their own defense.

Many people believe that chemicals produced by nature are safe and synthetic ones are harmful. They fear that synthetic chemicals will cause cancer and that any exposure to them must be dangerous. It is true that some synthetic chemicals cause cancer, and others are highly toxic. But it also is true that many synthetic chemicals are harmless at doses normally encountered in food, water, air, and other sources.

The same is true for natural chemicals—they range from relatively harmless to highly toxic. Some plants and animals create toxic chemicals called *toxins,* either for self-defense or for assistance in catching their prey. Think about rattlesnakes, scorpions, and poison ivy—each produces a natural toxin that is hazardous to humans as well as to other organisms in the environment.

The *dose* is the total amount of a chemical that an individual eats, drinks, breathes, or absorbs through the skin.

The distinction between synthetic and natural is not always clear-cut because people can manufacture many chemicals that occur in nature. For example, the vitamin C in an orange is identical to ascorbic acid created in a laboratory. There are additional benefits to eating an orange that you do not get from taking a vitamin C tablet, but the vitamin itself is identical from either source.

HOW MUCH IS TOO MUCH?

To measure a chemical's short-term toxicity, scientists carry out something called a "dose/response" study. The word *dose* refers to the total amount of a substance to which an individual is exposed through the mouth, lungs, or skin. Your total dose of a chemical includes the amount of the chemical that you eat, either by itself or contained in food or drinks, and the amount that you inhale with the air you breathe. It also includes absorption through your skin, which could happen if the chemical were dissolved in your bath water or included in your shampoo or skin care products. All of these sources together make up your *exposure* to the chemical.

Exposure means coming in contact with a chemical—through food, water, air, or other sources.

Exposure to a toxic chemical can be either intentional or unintentional. For example, a person who chooses to swallow too many pills is taking an intentional overdose. Someone who accidentally becomes poisoned by eating contaminated food receives an unintentional overdose. Similarly, a smoker intentionally inhales whatever substances are contained in cigarette smoke, whereas nearby people get exposed unintentionally when they inhale second-hand smoke.

The word *response* refers to the changes in living things caused by exposure to a specified chemical or mixture. Typically, the higher the concentration of a toxic compound, the more powerful its effect. Scientists study this relationship by carrying out dose/response experiments to determine the response of laboratory organisms to various doses of a test chemical.

Scientists measure *response*, the biological changes in living things caused by exposure to a toxic substance.

Dose/Response Bioassays

Dose/response experiments are called *bioassays* (the word *assay* means test, and *bio* is short for biological). For any given chemical, the question is, "How much is too much?" At low enough doses, the test organisms are not harmed and may even benefit. At high enough doses, they all die. For each chemical, there is an intermediate range in which some individuals will be affected and others will not.

A *bioassay* uses living things to determine chemical toxicity.

In a typical dose/response bioassay, laboratory rats are each fed a single dose of the chemical being tested. Some rats get an extremely high dose, and others receive doses ranging from moderate to very low. Exposure to the chemical occurs only on the first day, but the experiment continues for 14 days in order to give the organisms time to react. At the end of this period, scientists count the number of dead rats and note any health-related responses in those that are still alive. At the highest dose, it is likely that all of the rats will have died. At the lowest dose, most of the rats probably will have survived. If the experiment has been properly designed, there should be several doses that have killed some but not all of the exposed rats.

A *dose/response bioassay* measures "How much is too much?"

The end result is a number called the LD50, which stands for the lethal dose for 50% of the treated organisms. In other words, half of the rats that received the LD50 dose have died by the end of the 14-day test period. LD50s are expressed in terms of milligrams of the chemical per kilogram of body weight (mg/kg).

The *LD50* is the dose causing death of half of the organisms exposed at this level.

The experiment should also include a control group. The rats in the control group are treated exactly the same as the other rats except that they are not exposed to the chemical being tested—their dose of this chemical is zero.

Within any species, some individuals will die at lower doses than others. When rats are fed caffeine, some may die after eating only 100 mg, while others may tolerate 20 or 30 times this amount. Humans show these same kinds of differences. A cup of coffee at bedtime may have no effect on one person, yet may keep someone else awake through the whole night. Therefore, rather than relying on individuals, toxicity tests are based on group responses. The more individuals tested, the better the chance of accurately estimating the LD50 and of identifying low doses to which only the most sensitive individuals respond.

SCI*LINKS*.
THE WORLD'S A CLICK AWAY

**Topic: bioassays
Go to: www.sciLINKS.org
Code: ATR02**

FIGURE 1.1
A Typical Dose/Response Curve

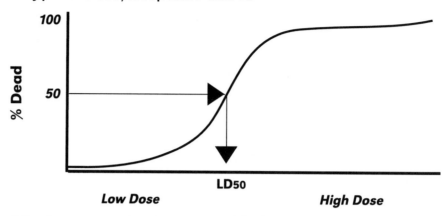

Follow the arrows to see how the percentage of deaths is used to figure out the LD50 (the dose representing death of 50% of the treated organisms).

Some individuals are more sensitive than others to any particular chemical.

LD50 experiments measure lethal dose—the amount of a chemical that will kill 50% of the test organisms. But of course chemical exposures can affect organisms in ways other than death, such as causing nausea, dizziness, skin rashes, or paralysis. When scientists carry out LD50 experiments, they also look for health effects such as these and record the doses at which such effects occur.

Comparing Chemical Toxicities

The more toxic the compound, the lower its LD50 . That makes sense if you think of poisons—the more poisonous a chemical is, the less it takes to kill you. For caffeine, the LD50 is roughly 200 mg in laboratory rats. For trichloroethylene, it is over 7,000 mg. This means that on average, rats can survive eating over 35 times as much pure trichloroethylene as caffeine. (This is a 14-day test and does not consider possible long-term impacts on health and survival.)

Even "Just a Taste" Can Be Too Much

It only took a little! This is the message behind the story of Loretta Boberg, a 62-year-old woman from Wisconsin who always tastes food before serving it to company. In this case, the company can be very thankful she did.

When Mrs. Boberg opened a jar of home-canned carrots last January, she dipped in a finger to taste the juice. Not liking the taste, she served home-canned beans to her guests instead. Within two days, Mrs. Boberg became dizzy and had difficulty walking. At first, hospital staff thought she had suffered a stroke because of her slurred speech and muscle weakness. The doctor did ask her if she had eaten any spoiled food lately, however. Too weak to speak, Mrs. Boberg wrote "carrots" on a piece of paper.

> If this physician had not suspected botulism, even though he had seen only a few cases, Mrs. Boberg would probably have died. The toxin moved through the respiratory system, paralyzing her muscles. A sample from the jar was fed to a laboratory mouse and it died instantly. The road to recovery for this lady was very slow.
>
> Mrs. Boberg used a boiling water canner for the carrots that gave her botulism. Yes, this was the same method she had used—and only by luck had gotten away with—for the past 44 years. This year she was not so lucky. If, like Mrs. Boberg, you are canning low-acid foods such as vegetables (except tomatoes), red meats, seafood, and poultry in a boiling water canner or by the open kettle method, you may wish to think twice before taking another chance...
> (*Andress 1991*)

Botulin, the compound that came close to killing Mrs. Boberg in the story above, is one of the most highly toxic chemicals known. It is created by bacteria in improperly canned foods. People eating these foods suffer a severe form of food poisoning called botulism. As you can tell by comparing LD_{50} values in Table 1.1, the compound that causes botulism is a million times more toxic than cyanide, and twenty million times more toxic than caffeine. In its pure form, less than one drop of botulin toxin is enough to kill 500 adult humans.

To get an idea what LD_{50} numbers mean, you can compare them to the amounts it would take to kill a typical human adult (see Table 1.2).

The LD_{50} values in Table 1.1 are based on experiments in which the compounds were fed to rats. LD_{50} values should always include information about the type of animal and how it was exposed to the chemical being tested. Otherwise, it is impossible to interpret what the values mean or to compare them to values reported by other scientists.

For some compounds, there is a big difference in LD_{50} values from one species to another. Dioxin is a good example. The LD_{50} for dioxin is 5,000 times higher for hamsters than for guinea pigs. How could this be? Many factors affect how sensitive each species will be to a particular compound. One of these factors is how the chemical gets metabolized. How much gets absorbed into the animal's blood, or stored in its liver, kidneys, or other tissues? How much passes right through and is excreted? How much gets converted into other chemical forms? The answers to these questions may vary from one species to another.

For example, a human being would have a hard time dying from eating too much chocolate. This is not true for dogs—eating just a few chocolate bars can be fatal to dogs because they cannot digest and break down the chemicals in chocolate in the same way that humans do.

Species may respond in different ways to toxic chemicals.

TABLE 1.1
Lethal Doses of Some Common Compounds

Substance	Comments	LD50* (mg/kg)
Botulin	An extremely toxic compound formed by bacteria in improperly canned foods; causes botulism, a sometimes fatal form of food poisoning	0.00001
Aflatoxin	A cancer-causing chemical created by mold on grains and nuts; can be found in some peanut butter and other nut and grain products	0.003
Cyanide	A highly poisonous substance found in apricot and cherry pits and used in industrial processes such as making plastics, electroplating, and producing chemicals	10
Vitamin D	An essential part of the human diet but toxic in doses higher than those found in normal human diets	10
Nicotine	The addictive agent that occurs naturally in tobacco and is added to some cigarettes to make them more addictive	50
Caffeine	A compound that occurs naturally in cocoa and coffee beans and is a common food additive	200
Acetylsalicylic acid	The active ingredient in aspirin	1,000
Sodium chloride	Table salt	3,000
Ethanol	Alcohol in beer, wine, and other intoxicating beverages	7,000
Trichloroethylene	A solvent and a common contaminant in groundwater and surface water supplies	7,200
Citric acid	An ingredient in citrus fruits such as oranges, grapefruits, and lemons	12,000
Sucrose	Sugar, refined from sugar cane or sugar beets	30,000

These LD50s are based on oral ingestion by rats. They represent single doses that cause death of 50% of the treated animals within 14 days of exposure. LD50s are expressed in terms of milligrams of the substance per kilogram of body weight (mg/kg).

TABLE 1.2
Toxicity Categories Used for Human Poisons

Toxicity Category	LD50 (mg/kg)	Probable Lethal Dose for 70 kg Human Adult	Example Compounds
Super toxic	<5	<0.35 g	Botulin Aflatoxin
Extremely toxic	5–50	0.35–3.5 g	Cyanide Vitamin D (calciferol)
Very toxic	50–500	3.5–35 g	Nicotine Caffeine
Moderately toxic	500–5,000	35–350 g	Aspirin (acetylsalicyclic acid) Salt (sodium chloride)
Slightly toxic	5,000–15,000	350–1,050 g	Ethanol Trichloroethylene
Practically nontoxic	>15,000	>1,050 g	Sugar (sucrose)

Many animals, including dogs and humans, will vomit if they eat something disagreeable. Rats and other rodents cannot vomit. Does this mean we should not use rodents in laboratory tests of chemical toxicity? Obviously they do not represent an exact model of how a person might respond to the same chemical. However, they do provide information that we can use to make limited conclusions about possible health effects on people.

Another concern related to use of laboratory animals for toxicity testing is the issue of animal rights. This is a complicated issue. Some people find it unethical to carry out experiments that may cause suffering or death of the test animals. However, we all want to be confident that we will not become sick, blind, or otherwise injured by the medicines, cleaning products, cosmetics, and huge range of other chemicals that we use on a daily basis.

Over the past few decades, scientists have developed a variety of new techniques to reduce the number of laboratory animals used in toxicology experiments. For example, some tests are carried out on single cells or on blood samples rather than on whole organisms. However, it has not been possible to eliminate the need for animal experiments. This is because there is no guarantee that the response of molecules, cells, or tissues will provide a reasonable model of the response of whole animals or humans.

The toxicity of a chemical depends on many factors, including whether it gets broken down, is stored in the body, or is excreted.

SCI LINKS.
THE WORLD'S A CLICK AWAY

Topic: animal experiments
Go to: *www.sciLINKS.org*
Code: ATR03

LONG-TERM VERSUS SHORT-TERM TOXICITY

For most of human history, concern about the toxic effects of chemicals has focused on poisons that cause a rapid death. The earliest descriptions of human life include stories about use of toxic plant and animal extracts—to coat arrows and spears used in hunting or fighting battles, or to create poisonous drinks used to kill prisoners. These are examples of *acute* toxicity, the effects of a single exposure to a toxic compound. LD50 experiments are designed to assess acute toxicity by measuring the short-term response of test organisms to a single dose of a chemical. Acute toxicity experiments provide useful information but give a limited view of overall toxicity because they address only short-term responses to single doses.

Acute effects are caused by exposure to a single dose, such as death caused by walking into a room filled with toxic fumes.

For some chemicals, the same total dose can be either deadly or harmless, depending on the rate of exposure. For other chemicals, this is not true, and even tiny doses can add up to toxic concentrations over time. This is because our liver and kidneys work to break down and get rid of toxic chemicals, but these systems work better for some types of chemicals than others.

Lead is an example of a chemical that builds up in our bodies over time rather than getting broken down or excreted. Lead poisoning has been linked with stunted growth and mental retardation in children. These are not sudden effects, but ones that develop gradually with long-term, low-level exposures to lead in air, food, and drinking water. Children living in homes with lead paint receive additional doses when they eat chips of paint or breathe dust-filled air. Even though the daily doses may be quite low, lead accumulates in bones. When the concentrations become too high, lead poisoning damages the nervous system and kidneys, causing problems such as hearing loss and mental retardation.

For many other types of chemicals, low daily doses do not cause problems such as these, and toxic effects occur only with short-term exposure to relatively large doses. For example, the oxalic acid found in rhubarb and spinach is harmless at the low concentrations found in these foods, but it would lead to kidney damage or death if you managed to eat 10 to 20 pounds of these foods at one meal.

Alcoholic drinks work the same way. A person who drinks too many drinks in a short period of time may die from acute alcohol poisoning. At the rate of only one drink per day, that same total amount of alcohol might do little or no harm. At this slower rate, most people's livers would have time to break down the alcohol rather than allowing it to build up to harmful levels in the body. However, "most people" does not include everyone, and there are some individuals with extra sensitivity to the toxic effects of any particular chemical. In the case of alcohol, pregnant women are cautioned not to drink because of the heightened sensitivity of their unborn children to alcohol toxicity.

Within limits, our bodies can break down or get rid of many types of toxic compounds before they harm our health. However, it is possible to expect too much of our bodies. With continued exposure to a toxic chemical, the liver can become damaged. Alcoholics frequently suffer from this problem, as do people who have had long-term exposure to toxic compounds through their work or through living in a contaminated environment.

In recent years, people have become increasingly concerned about the effects of long-term exposure to relatively low doses of contaminants. These are called *chronic* effects. If you lived in a house with a leaky furnace, you might be exposed to either acute or chronic carbon monoxide poisoning. Acute poisoning would occur if your house were tightly sealed, with so little ventilation that carbon monoxide fumes could build up to lethal levels. If your house were better ventilated, you would be more likely to suffer chronic effects such as headaches and fatigue from exposure to lower concentrations of the toxic fumes.

Chronic effects develop slowly due to long-term exposure to contaminants in water, food, or the environment.

TESTING CHRONIC TOXICITY

The easiest way to test chemical toxicity is to count how many test organisms suffer serious health effects or die when exposed to large doses. However, for most types of environmental pollution, these acute toxicity measurements do not provide answers to the questions we are interested in asking. For example, we might wonder whether it is harmful to drink water that contains low concentrations of a chemical such as trichloroethylene. The concentrations are not high enough to cause acute poisoning, but we would also want to know whether it might be dangerous to drink the water every day for many years. Would this cause a disease such as cancer or asthma? Would it result in birth defects, reduced growth rates, or lowered intelligence in children? These questions concern chronic toxicity.

Tests for chronic toxicity measure health problems rather than death rates.

To measure acute toxicity, you count how many test animals die within a couple of weeks after a single exposure to a chemical. For chronic toxicity, we want to know how the animals' health is affected by continuing exposure over a much longer time period. Rats, mice, or other lab animals are fed relatively low doses of the test chemical each day for months or years. During this time, the experimenters look for various effects such as lowered growth rates, changes in behavior, increased susceptibility to disease, or reduced ability to produce healthy young. Since lab animals lead much shorter lives than humans, it is possible to study effects on life span and reproduction without having to wait decades for the results.

In the case of trichloroethylene, chronic exposure has caused cancer as well as damage to the liver, kidneys, and central nervous system of laboratory animals. Whether trichloroethylene causes cancer in humans is still uncertain. Limited data are available on humans who have used trichloroethylene in poorly ventilated areas. These people have suffered from dizziness, headaches, slowed reaction time, sleepiness, and facial numbness. Data on the concentrations causing health effects such as these are used by the government in setting standards for acceptable chronic exposure to trichloroethylene through water, air, and other sources.

CONCLUSION

This chapter describes the process of measuring how a chemical affects laboratory animals such as rats. You may be wondering how data from these dose/response experiments can be used in the real world. For example, suppose that scientists have determined that rats tend to develop liver disease when exposed to a certain concentration of trichloroethylene in their daily diets. How can the government use this information in deciding the maximum concentration to allow in human drinking water?

Toxicity experiments provide the basis for government regulations that specify what concentrations of certain chemicals are allowed in human food, drinking water, drugs, and cosmetics. The next chapter explains how this process occurs, starting with laboratory data and ending with regulations about chemical use.

FOR DISCUSSION

▶ What do you think that Paracelsus meant when he wrote that the right dose differentiates a poison from a remedy? Can you think of a substance that is good for you at one dose and poisonous at another?

▶ Why might it be useful to know the LD_{50} for a chemical? How might you use this information?

▶ If a compound is shown to be practically nontoxic in a dose/response bioassay, can you conclude that this compound will have no toxic effects on living things? What other sorts of tests might be useful in helping you to make this decision?

TOXICITY CALCULATIONS

Name_____ Date_____

Based on the LD50 for caffeine (see Table 1.1), how many cups of coffee would you estimate that it would take to kill an average human of your size (assuming that humans respond in the same way as rats to this compound)? You can calculate this using the steps below:

1. Convert your weight to kilograms:

   _____ lbs × 0.45 kg/lb = _____ kg

2. Calculate the average lethal dose for a human your size:

   _____ mg/kg × _____ kg = _____ mg caffeine
   LD50   your weight

3. Assuming that each cup of coffee contains 90 mg caffeine,
   calculate how many cups it would take to kill an average person about your size:

   _____ mg caffeine ÷ 90 mg/cup = _____ cups of coffee

What Does This Number Mean?

A. Take a look at the number you calculated in Step 3. If you were to drink one cup of coffee per day for this number of days, would you be likely to die from an overdose of caffeine? Why or why not?

B. If you could drink exactly the number of cups of coffee you calculated in Step 3 all at one sitting, would you be guaranteed to die? Why or why not?

C. What is the most important assumption that we make when we use LD50s to estimate lethal doses for humans?

CHAPTER 2

FROM DATA TO STANDARDS

> When we turn on our taps, Americans expect the water that comes out to be clean and safe. Access to clean, safe water is fundamental to our quality of life.
>
> *Press Release from the White House, 1/17/01*

Everyone wants safe drinking water. But who decides what is "safe," and how is this decision made? If you were to conduct a public opinion poll, most people would probably tell you that they don't want any chemicals in their drinking water. This would in fact be impossible. Water itself is a chemical, made up of hydrogen and oxygen. In nature, all water contains additional chemicals such as calcium, magnesium, iron, and other minerals that dissolve as water flows past rocks and through soil. Human activities add many more chemicals to our water supplies.

All water in nature contains chemicals.

Some of the chemicals in water are relatively harmless, but others are considered contaminants because they cause problems when present at high enough concentrations. Water containing sulfur compounds is unpleasant to drink because it smells and tastes like rotten eggs. Water high in iron leaves rusty-looking stains on sinks, toilets, and bathtubs, and water with high copper concentrations leaves blue stains on plumbing fixtures. However, many dissolved substances have no noticeable color, odor, or taste. Since you can't rely on taste or other sensory cues to indicate what is in your water, how can you tell if your water is safe to drink?

SETTING DRINKING WATER STANDARDS

If your water comes from a public water supply, it must meet standards set by the federal government. The federal Safe Drinking Water Act requires the Environmental Protection Agency (EPA) to regulate drinking water contaminants to protect public health.

Drinking water standards are designed to protect people from daily chemical exposures over their entire lives.

The concentrations of contaminants in drinking water rarely are high enough to cause acute poisoning. Instead, the concern of health officials is to make sure that the concentrations are low enough to protect people from

TABLE 1.3
Maximum Contaminant Levels Set by EPA for Selected Chemicals in U.S.
Public Water Supplies

Substance	Sources of Contaminant in Drinking Water	Potential Health Effects to Humans from Contaminated Water	Maximum Contaminant Level (mg/L)*
Dioxin	Emissions from waste incineration and other combustion; discharge from chemical factories	Reproductive difficulties; liver damage; increased risk of cancer	0.00000003
PCBs	Runoff from landfills and hazardous waste sites; former manufacture and disposal of electrical transformers, electromagnets, fluorescent lights, and plastics	Skin problems; thymus gland problems; immune deficiencies; reproductive or nervous system difficulties; increased risk of cancer	0.0005
Trichloroethylene	Wastewater from metal degreasing and finishing operations and from paint, ink, electrical components, and rubber processing industries	Liver and kidney damage; increased risk of cancer	0.005
Mercury	Erosion of natural deposits; discharge from refineries and factories; runoff from landfills and cropland	Brain and nerve damage; kidney damage; birth defects; skin rash	0.002
Lead	Corrosion of household plumbing systems; disposal of storage batteries; industrial discharges; erosion of natural deposits	Kidney problems; high blood pressure; delays in physical or mental development of infants and children	0.015
Trihalomethanes	Produced by chemical reactions in water that has been disinfected with chlorine	Liver, kidney, or central nervous system problems; increased risk of cancer	0.1
Cyanide	Discharge from metal, plastic, and fertilizer factories	Nerve damage or thyroid problems	0.2
Nitrate	Runoff of fertilizer and manure; sewage; leaching from septic tanks	Methemoglobinemia ("blue baby syndrome") in infants under 6 months old	10.0

* Maximum Contaminant Levels are expressed in terms of milligrams of the chemical per liter of water (mg/L).

chronic health effects such as cancer, birth defects, or damage to the liver or other organs. The goal is to set standards that enable people to safely drink the water for an entire lifetime.

For each contaminant, EPA must establish a national drinking water standard, called a Maximum Contaminant Level, to be used for all public water supplies. So far, EPA has established these standards for over 80 contaminants, including naturally occurring substances as well as synthetic compounds such as PCBs and pesticides. A few examples are listed in Table 1.3.

The Maximum Contaminant Level for lead is 0.015 mg/L (Table 1.3). Does this mean that you would get sick or die if you were to drink a glass of water with a slightly higher concentration? No, this number simply is an estimate of the maximum concentration that an average person could drink every day over a period of many years without developing related health problems. If higher concentrations are measured in a public water supply, the supplier must notify the public and might also be required to provide alternative drinking water supplies.

Establishing drinking water standards is a complicated process that involves a combination of scientific data and human judgment. For each chemical, the first step is to look at all of the available toxicological data. For most chemicals, dose/response data are not available for humans because it would be unethical to expose people to chemical doses that might be harmful, just for the sake of studying the potential effects. Therefore, dose/response data from laboratory animals must be used to estimate potential effects on humans.

Setting standards requires data and judgment.

Think back to the LD_{50} values used to express acute toxicity. Each LD_{50} represents the amount of a substance needed to kill 50% of the laboratory rats or other test animals within two weeks of receiving a single dose. An LD_{50} is a relatively easy number to come up with, but it doesn't tell us what we need to know for setting drinking water standards for humans. A more relevant question would be, "What dose could rats eat or drink every day for a lifetime without causing health problems?" To come up with these estimates, scientists study the chronic effects of lower concentrations of the test chemical on the health and survival rates of laboratory animals. If data exist for more than one type of animal, the most sensitive species is chosen.

But how can animal bioassay data be used in determining an acceptable concentration of any particular chemical in human drinking water? Answering this question involves carrying out a series of calculations based on questions such as those in Table 1.4.

In setting drinking water standards for most chemicals, EPA uses an average adult male weighing 70 kg (154 lb) who drinks two liters of water each day throughout a 70-year lifetime. Clearly we are not all 70 kg adult males, but this generalization is used for calculation purposes. If any subgroup of humans is known to be particularly sensitive to the chemical in question, then the standard is set with this sensitivity in mind. For example, the 10 mg/L drinking water standard for nitrate is based on the fact that infants are more

SCI LINKS
THE WORLD'S A CLICK AWAY

Topic: drinking water standards
Go to: www.sciLINKS.org
Code: ATR04

TABLE 1.4
Questions Used in Converting from Animal Data to Human Drinking Water Standards

Topic	Question
Human characteristics	▶ How much does the average person weigh? ▶ How much water does the average person drink per day? ▶ How long is the average human life?
Chemical characteristics	▶ How much of this chemical are humans exposed to through other sources, such as eating, breathing, or absorbing it through the skin while bathing or swimming? ▶ Does this chemical accumulate in the human body or is it quickly broken down or excreted? ▶ Is this chemical believed to cause cancer in humans? ▶ Do males react differently to this chemical than females? ▶ How might a baby, elderly person, or person with a weakened immune system react differently to this chemical than the "average" person?
Data characteristics	▶ What uncertainty factors should be used in translating between the measured effects of this chemical in laboratory animals and its estimated effects in humans?

sensitive than adults to nitrate concentrations. (Excess nitrate can cause "blue baby syndrome," which lowers the ability of a baby's blood to carry oxygen.)

As you can see from the list of questions in Table 1.4, many assumptions and judgments must be made to convert from data on laboratory animals to an estimate of health effects of a particular chemical on humans. Obviously, there is a lot of uncertainty involved in this process.

An ***uncertainty factor*** is used to correct for differences between experimental animals and humans.

The *uncertainty factor* is a number that is used to provide a margin of safety in the calculations. Let's use a simple example. Suppose that lab tests showed that mice could eat up to 200 mg of a chemical per kilogram of body weight with no signs of illness. Instead of using 200 mg/kg as the safe dose of this chemical for humans, EPA would divide this number by an uncertainty factor. Using an uncertainty factor of 100, for example, the 200 mg/kg safe dose for mice would be reduced to just 2 mg/kg for humans:

$$200 \text{ mg/kg} \div 100 = 2 \text{ mg/kg}$$

safe	uncertainty	adjusted
dose	factor	safe dose
in mice		for humans

In setting drinking water standards, EPA chooses an uncertainty factor ranging anywhere from 10 to 1000. Which number is chosen depends on EPA's confidence that the available data provide an accurate estimate of the chemical's effects on human health. An uncertainty factor of 10 is chosen only when valid data are available on acute and chronic exposures to humans. When human data are not available, higher uncertainty factors are used.

FROM DATA TO STANDARDS

As an example of the types of calculations EPA uses to convert from lab data to drinking water standards, let's take a theoretical chemical named Compound A. Suppose that 200 mg/kg/day is the highest dose of Compound A causing no observed long-term health problems in laboratory rats.

The first step is to apply the appropriate uncertainty factor. In this case we will use a factor of 100 because a complete set of data on acute and chronic toxicity is available for rats but not for humans, and we are reasonably confident that rats provide a good model of human response for this compound.

$$200 \text{ mg/kg/day} \div 100 = 2 \text{ mg/kg/day}$$

safe dose	uncertainty	adjusted
in rats	factor	safe dose

The next step is to convert this number into the amount per day for humans rather than rats. For this calculation, EPA uses 70 kg as the average weight of a male adult.

$$2 \text{ mg/kg/day} \times 70 \text{ kg} = 140 \text{ mg/day}$$

adjusted	weight of	comparable dose
safe dose	avg. human	in humans
	male adult	

Next we ask, "If all of this 140 mg/day were consumed in drinking water, what would the concentration be?" For this calculation, EPA assumes that the average person drinks 2 liters (L) of water per day.

$$140 \text{ mg/day} \div 2 \text{ L/day} = 70 \text{ mg/L}$$

But drinking water is not likely to be the only source of human exposure to Compound A. There may be some in our food, or in the air we breathe. Unless specific data are available on these other sources, EPA assumes that water represents only 20% of our daily consumption of any particular compound. Therefore, we need to reduce the amount allowed in water to make up for possible exposures from other sources.

$$70 \text{ mg/L} \times 0.20 = 14 \text{ mg/L}$$

If Compound A is not suspected of causing cancer in humans, 14 mg/L would be EPA's estimate of the amount of Compound A that would be safe to allow in human drinking water on a daily basis.

Before establishing this number as a human drinking water standard, EPA first would investigate whether any groups of humans have heightened sensitivity or exposure to this particular compound. They also would carry out a feasibility study to determine whether it is technically and financially feasible to provide water that meets the desired goal. The final step would be to combine the results of the health and feasibility studies to set the Maximum Contaminant Level, a legal drinking water standard that comes as close as possible to the health-based goal.

For chemicals that are known or suspected to cause cancer in humans, a different approach is used. For these compounds, no amount is considered acceptable in drinking water. However, a zero concentration cannot be measured, so the Maximum Contaminant Level is set at the lowest concentration that is feasible to measure.

Nothing is absolutely safe.

No one can guarantee that water meeting the standards will be absolutely safe to drink, or that there will be any harm in drinking water containing contaminants at concentrations exceeding the standards. However, the drinking water standards derived through the process described above represent careful judgments about what concentrations of various chemicals should be permitted in public drinking water supplies. EPA can revise the standards if updated scientific data indicate that a different level is more appropriate.

Keep in mind that drinking water standards will not protect every individual from any chance of harm. Instead, the standards are designed to provide an acceptable level of risk to the public as a whole. Because nothing is 100% safe, the idea of providing a safe water supply really means deciding what level of risk should be allowed. The concept of risk is discussed further in the next chapter.

FOR DISCUSSION

▶ EPA's maximum contaminant level for cyanide in drinking water is 0.2 mg/L. Do you think you would get sick if you drank a liter of water containing 0.3 mg/L of cyanide? Why or why not?

▶ How much uncertainty do you think is involved in setting drinking water standards? Would it be possible to collect enough scientific data to eliminate this uncertainty?

▶ Some people are more sensitive than others to any particular chemical. How does the standard-setting process take this into account?

CHAPTER 3

WHAT'S THE RISK?

Is diet soda safe to drink, or will it cause cancer? How important is it to use a seat belt while riding in a car, or to wear a helmet while motorcycling, bicycling, or skiing? These questions relate to *risk*, the chance that harm will occur under a certain set of conditions. We all make many decisions based on our ideas about risk.

Risk is the probability that something harmful will happen.

Let's take a simple example. Suppose that you want to travel to a distant city, but you are worried about getting there safely. You've heard about so many plane crashes recently that you're feeling hesitant to fly. You could lower your risk of being in a plane accident by deciding to drive instead. But does this make sense?

To make an informed decision on risk, you would want to compare the risk of airline travel to the risks of any other possible travel options. You might be surprised to learn that flying is actually less risky than driving. Many people feel safer behind the wheel of a car than as a passenger in an airplane but, in fact, for each mile of travel your risk of dying in an accident is higher in a car than a plane. How much higher? That depends on a wide range of factors, including the type of car or plane, the distance to be covered, and the experience and degree of alertness of the driver or pilot.

Nothing is absolutely safe, so there is no zero risk.

What if you were to decide that the risks just aren't worth it, so you will stay home rather than travel at all? Believe it or not, your risk still would not be zero—think of all the various types of accidents that could occur at home or in your neighborhood.

News stories frequently cover controversies concerning the safety of food or drinking water. Is it safe to eat food containing artificial colors, flavors, or preservatives? How about fruits or vegetables containing traces of pesticide residues? Should fluoride be added to drinking water to protect against tooth decay? All of these questions relate to *chemical risk*, the chance that you will experience health problems as a result of exposure to a particular chemical.

Chemical risk is the probability of harm caused by chemical exposures.

Some chemical risk decisions are personal choices. Is it worth becoming a smoker, knowing that you will face an increased risk of lung cancer because of exposure to cancer-causing chemicals in the smoke? This is a matter of individual choice. Other chemical risk decisions are made by the federal

Acceptable risk is determined using scientific data and human judgment.

government. For example, information about chemical risk provides the basis for regulations such as the drinking water standards discussed in Chapter 2. These standards represent estimates of safe concentrations of each chemical. But remember, nothing is absolutely safe, so the real question is what level of risk is acceptable?

Of course, what you consider to be an acceptable risk may be totally unacceptable to someone else. That may be fine when it relates to an individual decision such as whether to try skydiving. It gets more complicated when risk decisions apply to groups rather than individuals. People generally are more willing to accept voluntary risks than risks over which they have no control. For example, you might decide to try skydiving because you expect the thrill to be worth the risk. At the same time, you might become outraged when you hear that a major airline is cutting back on safety measures in order to cut costs. Although skydiving carries a higher risk of injury than riding as an airline passenger, the skydiving risk may be more acceptable to you because it is one over which you have personal choice and control.

Controversies over safety of food, air, or drinking water focus on issues of how much and what types of risk are acceptable to the general public. Through a process called *risk assessment*, scientists and politicians work together to try to answer these questions.

HOW SAFE IS SAFE ENOUGH?

The goal of **risk assessment** is to decide how safe is safe enough.

Is there reason to panic if trichloroethylene has been found in your town's water supply? What if the measured concentrations are below the drinking water standard for this compound? Should you stop eating peanut butter because you have heard that it contains a natural chemical called aflatoxin, which is known to cause cancer in laboratory animals? Synthetic compounds with long names like trichloroethylene sound dangerous, but how can you tell if they are any riskier than the wide range of compounds that are found naturally in food and water? Risk assessment is the process through which comparisons such as these can be made.

In assessing the risk to human health from exposure to chemicals, two basic questions need to be addressed:

▶ What health problems could this chemical cause?

▶ How likely are these health problems to occur?

For any particular chemical, risk assessment can be summarized with the equation:

> **Chemical Risk = Toxicity × Exposure**

Toxicity indicates what health problems are associated with various doses or concentrations. It is estimated using animal data (see **Dose/Response Bioassays** in Chapter 1) as well as any available data on effects on humans.

Exposure is an estimate of how much of the chemical a person is likely to eat, drink, or absorb from water, air, or other sources.

It is easy to assume that an extremely toxic chemical must also have a very high chemical risk, but this is not necessarily true. Take another look at the chemical risk equation—it includes exposure as well as toxicity. This means that the risk will be greatest if the chemical is highly toxic *and* people are exposed to it in significant amounts.

Suppose that a chemical is highly toxic but it breaks down into harmless compounds just minutes after being created in a laboratory. Risk to the public from this chemical would be extremely low in spite of its high toxicity. This particular chemical would pose great risk only to people working in or very near the laboratory where it is created, because these people are the only ones exposed to it during its short period of toxicity.

Many of the cleaning products that we use in our homes are highly toxic but they pose little risk to us because we are not tempted to eat or drink them. Young children are at much greater risk of being poisoned by these products because they don't know enough to keep them out of their mouths. By storing cleaning products in locked cabinets, we can greatly reduce the chemical risk to young children. This is an example of *risk management*—we haven't changed the toxicity of the cleaning products, but we have greatly reduced the chance for exposure among the types of people who are most likely to be affected.

WHAT ARE THE TRADE-OFFS?

Risk management involves making choices and setting priorities concerning safety, convenience, and cost. How safe is safe enough? How important is convenience compared with safety? How much money is it worth spending to reduce the risk?

Using the example of the household cleaning products, if you live by yourself you might decide that it is too expensive or inconvenient to keep your drain cleaner in a locked cabinet. A parent of young children, however, would be more likely to put up with the expense and inconvenience in order to decrease the risk of accidental poisoning.

One Risk versus Another

In many cases, risk decisions involve trade-offs between one type of risk versus another. For example, seven people in the New York City area died in 1999 after being bitten by mosquitoes infected with the West Nile virus. This virus had not previously been seen in the United States, and health officials suddenly were faced with the need to learn more about it and to prevent its spread before more people became infected. Government officials chose several risk management tactics, including teaching people how to protect themselves from mosquito bites. The most controversial part of the program was pesticide spraying to kill mosquitoes.

Without exposure, even a highly toxic chemical poses little risk.

Risk management involves making choices among safety, convenience, and cost.

SCI**LINKS**
THE WORLD'S A CLICK AWAY

Topic: West Nile virus
Go to: www.sciLINKS.org
Code: ATR05

Topic: stream/river
       pollution
Go to: www.sciLINKS.org
Code: ATR06

Throughout New York and New England, governments in affected towns and cities faced the difficult decision of whether to spray pesticides or to rely instead on other mosquito control options. In making this decision, health officials were forced to estimate which risk would be greater: the potential short- and long-term effects from pesticide exposure, or the more immediate prospect of human fatalities from this new insect-borne disease. Any public health decision such as this is likely to be highly controversial because different people will reach different conclusions about acceptable levels of risk from chemicals compared with disease or other factors.

During the summer of 2000, many towns and cities did use pesticides to limit the spread of West Nile virus. Was this the right choice? Science alone cannot answer this question. Scientific data provide useful estimates of the potential risks posed by West Nile virus compared with the potential risks caused by pesticide spraying. However, human judgment plays a key role in balancing these opposing risks and determining which risk management option to choose.

Chlorination of drinking water is another example of the need to weigh one risk against another in the protection of public health. In the 1800s, many people died from cholera, typhoid fever, and dysentery. People had not yet learned that germs in human sewage cause these diseases, and it was common for outhouses to hang right over the same streams that were also used for human drinking water.

By the early 1900s, people were attempting to keep untreated sewage out of their water supplies. They also had learned to disinfect public drinking water with chlorine to kill disease-causing organisms. As a consequence, deaths due to typhoid and other water-borne diseases were practically eliminated in the United States and many other parts of the world. However, in developing countries where water chlorination still is uncommon, 25 million people die each year from drinking unsafe water. Roughly one-quarter of all hospital beds worldwide are filled with patients who are sick from drinking or bathing in contaminated water.

Using chlorine to disinfect drinking water supplies clearly benefits human health and safety. However, adding chlorine to water is not a perfect solution. The water in rivers and streams usually contains natural acids that form when leaves and other organic materials decompose. In addition to killing germs, chlorine in the water also combines with these natural acids to form compounds called trihalomethanes (THMs). Chloroform is a THM that has been found in water supplies and it causes cancer in laboratory animals at high doses. If you could prove that THMs cause cancer in humans in the low concentrations commonly found in drinking water, how would you weigh the slim chance of getting cancer sometime during your lifetime versus the much greater probability of immediately coming down with a germ-caused disease such as cholera or typhoid fever?

Risk management decisions such as this require combining scientific data with human judgment to balance and minimize risks to human health.

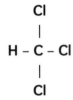

Cl
|
H – C – Cl
|
Cl

Chloroform is a common THM formed through the combination of chlorine with natural acids in water.

Often there is more than one possible solution. For example, scientists and engineers have been testing ways of reducing the formation of THMs in chlorinated water. They also have developed alternative methods to disinfect water, such as treatment with ultraviolet light or ozone instead of chlorine.

Risk versus Cost

Cost is another factor to consider in risk management. It is easy to say that you don't want THMs in your drinking water, but how much extra are you willing to pay for an alternate form of disinfection? This same sort of risk/cost trade-off also is important in public decisions about environmental quality.

For example, if a hazardous waste site were found in your community it might seem obvious that the toxic wastes should be removed. However, an important question is "How clean is clean enough?" Many factors are involved in planning an environmental cleanup operation. When EPA is involved, it begins the risk assessment process by asking the following questions:

▶ What contaminants exist at the site?

▶ How are people exposed to them?

▶ How dangerous could the contaminants be to human health?

▶ What contaminant concentrations are considered acceptable?

Although it is tempting to say that you want the soil to get completely purified so that no trace of contamination remains, it might be quite expensive to accomplish this ambitious goal. The closer you try to come to total contaminant removal, the greater the cost is likely to be (Figure 1.2).

FIGURE 1.2
Cost of Environmental Cleanup Depends on the Desired Level of Purity

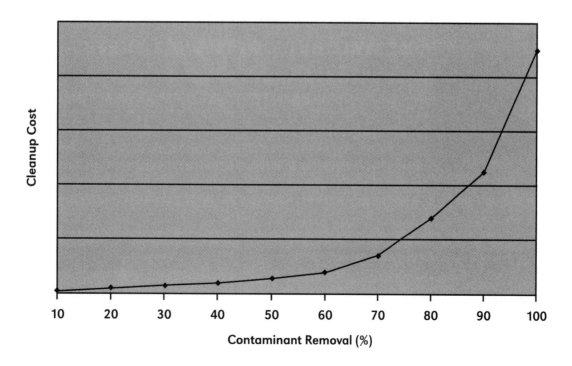

Chemical risk decisions rarely are simple or easy. Which are the highest priority risks? How can we best reduce these with the limited amount of money available? Although it is tempting to say that we want our food and water to be safe and our environment to be clean, inevitably there will be trade-offs in trying to meet these goals.

Through a combination of scientific analysis and human judgment, risk assessment provides a tool for figuring out which problems are most worth worrying about. Risk management then helps us to evaluate approaches, set priorities, and choose the best approaches for keeping risks within acceptable bounds.

FOR DISCUSSION

▶ Describe why the process of setting drinking water standards can be considered a form of chemical risk management.

▶ Think of an example of a chemical risk that you consider unacceptable. Do you know anyone else who would consider this same risk to be OK? If so, what kinds of laws or policies do you think would be appropriate for regulating this risk, and how should these regulations reflect differences in opinions about what level of risk is acceptable?

▶ Why is human judgment needed in setting drinking water standards? Explain why scientific data do not necessarily make it obvious what the standards should be.

▶ Can you think of a time when you have had to decide between one kind of risk and another? How about a trade-off between a risk and the cost of avoiding or minimizing it?

CHAPTER 4

ECOLOGICAL RISKS

So far we have been thinking about the effects of chemicals on human health and safety. Another important consideration is the impact of chemicals on the environment. What happens when fertilizers and pesticides drain from lawns, golf courses, and agricultural fields into nearby streams? What are the effects of automobile exhaust or the gases that come out of smokestacks at power plants, incinerators, and factories? Chemical releases into the environment affect not only human health, but also the health of plants, animals, and the ecosystems in which they live.

Chemical pollution was not a matter of widespread public concern until the 1960s, when Rachel Carson's classic book *Silent Spring* served as a wake-up call to Americans:

> On the mornings that had once throbbed with the dawn chorus of robins, catbirds, doves, jays, wrens, and scores of other bird voices there was now no sound; only silence lay over the fields and woods and marsh. No witchcraft, no enemy action had silenced the rebirth of new life in this stricken world. The people had done it themselves.
> *(Carson 1962)*

Rachel Carson wrote *Silent Spring* to focus public attention on the environmental impacts of DDT and similar pesticides. During World War II, DDT was widely regarded as a miraculous pesticide. Sprayed on swamps and other insect-breeding areas, it saved millions of human lives by reducing the spread of malaria, typhus, and other insect-borne diseases. DDT also was dusted directly on soldiers, refugees, and prisoners to kill lice and other insect pests. Because powdered DDT is not easily absorbed through skin, it seemed harmless. After the war, use of DDT for insect control in the United States grew by leaps and bounds.

In 1954 scientists at Michigan State University noticed that many robins on campus were dying. The cause turned out to be DDT poisoning. Although the birds may not have been exposed to DDT directly, it was present in the worms and insects that made up their diet (Figure 1.3). The campus trees had been sprayed with DDT to kill beetles and prevent the spread of

FIGURE 1.3
Buildup of DDT Concentrations
through Diets of Birds

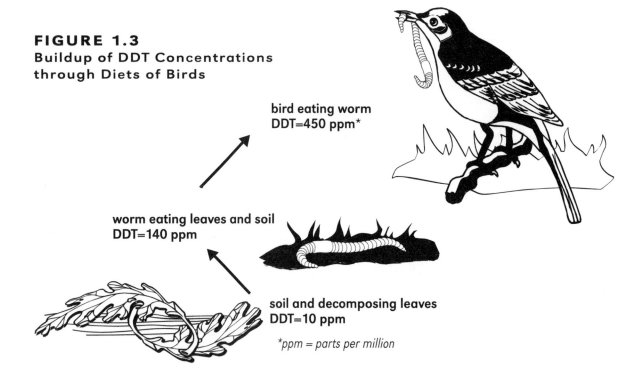

bird eating worm
DDT=450 ppm*

worm eating leaves and soil
DDT=140 ppm

soil and decomposing leaves
DDT=10 ppm

ppm = parts per million

Dutch elm disease. As worms and insects ate the decomposing leaves, DDT built up in their bodies. Some robins died from eating these worms and insects. Others developed problems with reproduction—either they failed to lay eggs, or they laid eggs with shells so thin that they cracked. Similar problems occurred with fish-eating birds including eagles, ospreys, and gulls.

Rachel Carson's title, *Silent Spring,* referred to a widespread decline in bird populations due to these deaths and reproduction problems. Because of damage to wildlife and potential threats to human health, in 1972 EPA banned use of DDT in the United States except in the case of public health emergencies.

EFFECTS OF CHEMICAL PROPERTIES

Scientists discovered several chemical properties that help to explain DDT's unexpected buildup in birds and other wildlife. One of these properties is the slow rate at which DDT breaks down. Through physical, chemical, and biological *degradation*, compounds decompose into simpler compounds. When exposed to sunlight, moisture, and warmth, some chemicals will degrade quickly. Because DDT degrades extremely slowly, it remains in the environment for many years and continues to make its way into the food of birds and other organisms (Figure 1.3).

Another important property of DDT is that it dissolves much more readily in fat or oil than in water. Once absorbed into the bodies of animals, DDT gets stored in fat and continues to accumulate over the years. This helps to explain why DDT concentrations tend to be low in water but much higher in the bodies of fish, birds, and mammals. This process is called *bioaccumulation*.

Through *degradation*, chemicals break down into simpler forms.

Bioaccumulation causes some chemicals to concentrate in animal fat.

Through *biomagnification*, these compounds build up to higher concentrations at each level of the food chain. In aquatic ecosystems, these processes start with tiny organisms called plankton. When plankton store DDT in their bodies, they concentrate it at levels higher than those in the surrounding water. Minnows and other small fish eat the plankton, and they continue the process of concentration by storing DDT in their fat cells. As these fish get eaten by larger fish, which then get eaten by birds, the concentrations continue to rise (Figure 1.4).

Through ***biomagnification***, some chemicals build up through the food chain.

FIGURE 1.4
Biomagnification of DDT through Aquatic Food Chains

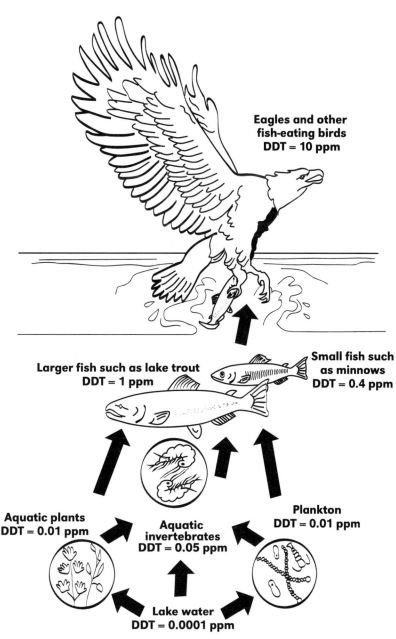

Eagles and other fish-eating birds
DDT = 10 ppm

Larger fish such as lake trout
DDT = 1 ppm

Small fish such as minnows
DDT = 0.4 ppm

Aquatic plants
DDT = 0.01 ppm

Aquatic invertebrates
DDT = 0.05 ppm

Plankton
DDT = 0.01 ppm

Lake water
DDT = 0.0001 ppm

Some chemicals *adsorb* to soil particles.

DDT was the first pesticide to surprise people with unforeseen environmental consequences, but it has not been the only one. In the late 1970s, a pesticide called aldicarb was found in wells used for drinking water by hundreds of families on Long Island, New York. Aldicarb was being used to protect potato crops from the Colorado potato beetle but was not expected to *leach*, or wash out of the soil and into the groundwater. Until the 1940s, most pesticides were compounds of arsenic, mercury, copper, or lead. It is still possible to measure high concentrations of these compounds in the soil of old orchards and farm fields. Instead of breaking down or leaching out of the soil, these compounds *adsorb*, or get tightly bound to soil particles. Initial tests for aldicarb indicated that it would adsorb to soil and break down into less toxic chemical forms.

How then did aldicarb find its way into the wells of Long Island? The unexpected contamination occurred because Long Island's light, sandy soils allowed aldicarb to leach downward to groundwater rather than remaining in the topsoil and gradually breaking down.

Chemicals that dissolve in water may *leach* or wash out of the soil.

Another environmental surprise occurred in the discovery of an insecticide named toxaphene in the bodies of fish and wildlife in the Arctic and northern regions. During the 1960s and 1970s, toxaphene was heavily used to control insect pests on cotton and other crops in the southern United States and other countries. In 1982 EPA banned the use of toxaphene on U.S. crops because of its effects on human and animal health.

How did toxaphene get hundreds, even thousands of miles from where it had been used? Studies have shown that toxaphene evaporates and gets carried by wind, and then rainfall brings it back down to earth. Because it breaks down very slowly, it persists a long time in the environment. The result is that even today, long after its use was discontinued, toxaphene continues to be carried by wind to all parts of the globe (Figure 1.5).

TESTING ENVIRONMENTAL IMPACTS OF NEW COMPOUNDS

Because of what we have learned from experience with pesticides such as DDT, aldicarb, and toxaphene, new pesticide compounds now get subjected to a more thorough scientific review, focusing on questions such as the following:

▶ How rapidly does it break down?

▶ Does it dissolve better in water or in oil?

▶ How quickly does it evaporate?

▶ Does it bind to soil particles or leach out as water percolates through?

▶ Does it tend to build up in fish, birds, and other wildlife?

▶ How toxic is it to humans and to organisms in the environment?

Pesticides are just one example of chemicals that humans introduce into the environment. Of course there are many others—detergents, solvents, and industrial waste products, to name just a few. The Toxic Substances Control

FIGURE 1.5
Movement and Fates of Pesticides in the Environment

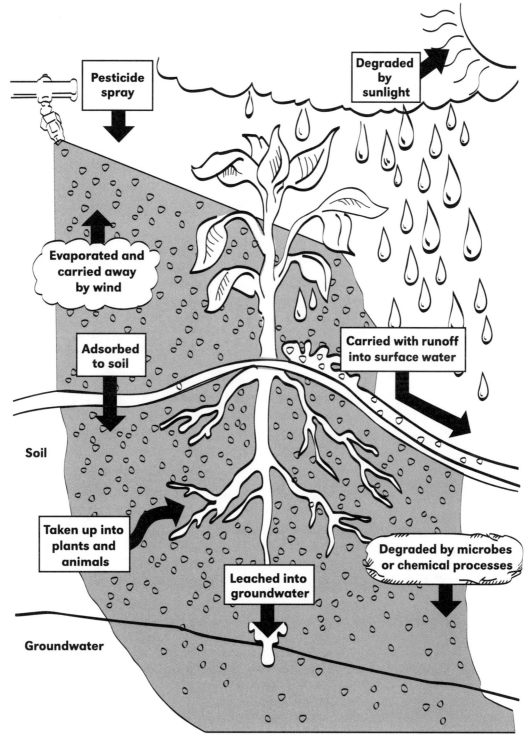

Act, enacted by Congress in 1976, authorizes EPA to track the 75,000 industrial chemicals currently in use in the United States.

EPA screens these chemicals and can require testing of any that appear likely to cause hazards to human or environmental health. Unfortunately, thorough testing is both time-consuming and expensive, and very few of the products currently on the market have gone through this sort of review.

FOR DISCUSSION

▶ Why didn't scientists anticipate that DDT would cause problems in the environment?

▶ Suppose that you are developing a new pesticide to limit the amount of damage that beetles cause to apple trees. Much of your research will focus on the ability of this compound to protect apple crops, but what else will you need to consider? What properties would you hope to find in a chemical that will be applied to orchards and home gardens?

CHAPTER 5

USING BIOASSAYS FOR ENVIRONMENTAL RESEARCH

When scientists want to determine the possible impacts of a substance on human health, they conduct dose/response bioassays using rats, mice, or other laboratory animals (Chapter 1). The results are expressed as LD50 values, which describe the lethal dose that kills 50% of the exposed organisms within a specified period of time. Scientists use these bioassay results to compare the toxicity of various compounds and to predict potential effects on human health and safety.

Another use of bioassays is to determine chemical toxicity related to potential environmental impacts. For example, scientists use bioassays to test the toxicity of environmental samples such as water from lakes, streams, or runoff ditches. Instead of using laboratory rats or mice, in this case it makes sense to conduct bioassays with organisms that are typical of the environment being tested. Examples include fish, aquatic invertebrates, worms, and single-celled algae.

Environmental bioassays are used to test the toxicity of mixtures of chemicals such as wastewater from industries or sewage treatment plants. These facilities have permits that specify maximum concentrations of specific chemicals they are allowed to discharge into a lake, stream, or other water body. Sometimes the permits also require periodic bioassays in order to test the combined toxicity of all the chemicals present in each wastewater sample.

Another way in which bioassays are used for environmental testing is to investigate hazardous waste sites. For example, at the Rocky Mountain Arsenal in Colorado, the ground in some areas is highly contaminated with pesticides and various warfare chemicals. In order to plan the cleanup operation, scientists began by testing soil samples with lettuce seed bioassays. Using these simple and inexpensive tests, they were able to create maps showing the areas in greatest need of cleanup. The more expensive chemical

Dose/response bioassays using rats or mice help scientists estimate toxicity to humans.

SCi*LINKS*
THE WORLD'S A CLICK AWAY

Topic: sewage treatment
Go to: www.sciLINKS.org
Code: ATR08

analyses then could be targeted to the most highly contaminated regions, and the results were used to plan appropriate cleanup strategies.

BIOASSAY SPECIES

This book presents protocols for bioassays using three types of organisms: *Daphnia*, duckweed, and lettuce seeds. With each of these, you expose the test organisms to a chemical solution or environmental sample, and then measure how the organisms respond compared with the control group that has not been exposed.

Daphnia are tiny crustaceans that are related to lobsters and crabs, but look more like fleas as they hop in water. In bioassays using *Daphnia*, you can measure acute toxicity by counting how many individuals have died after two days.

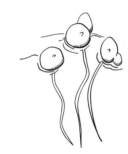

Duckweed is a small plant that floats on the surface of ponds and lakes. In duckweed bioassays, you float the plants on the surface of chemical solutions or water samples, then measure their growth and observe their health after five days.

In **lettuce seed** bioassays, you place seeds in petri dishes containing chemical solutions or samples of water, sediment, or soil. At the end of a five-day growth period you count how many seeds have sprouted; measure the length of any roots that have grown; and note any distortions in their shape, color, or appearance. Since you wouldn't expect to find lettuce growing in the wild, lettuce seeds may seem an odd choice for bioassays of environmental samples. The reason they are used for this purpose is that they are known to be sensitive to common environmental contaminants such as heavy metals and some types of pesticides, solvents, and other organic compounds.

You may be wondering how scientists choose what types of bioassay organisms to use in their experiments. In general, the species used for bioassays should be sensitive to various types of chemicals and chemical mixtures. They also should be relatively easy to keep alive in a laboratory. No single species provides the perfect bioassay. Each responds in its own way, so toxicity testing usually includes more than one species in order to provide a more complete picture of toxicity.

The choice of which organisms to use depends on the purpose of the bioassays. For bioassays designed to estimate toxicity to humans, organisms such as laboratory rats and mice commonly are used because their response to chemical exposures provides a reasonable model of human response. For environmental bioassays, the species of choice may depend on the type of chemicals being studied and the purpose of the experiments. For example, suppose that you want to investigate potential environmental impacts of herbicides that are used to kill weeds in lakes and ponds. Using bioassays with lettuce seeds, duckweed, and possibly other types of aquatic vegetation, you could determine whether the herbicide is specific to certain types of weeds, or is toxic to plants in general.

You might also be interested in investigating the toxicity of the herbicide to nontarget species such as the fish and wildlife living in lakes and ponds. Of the three bioassay species presented in this book, *Daphnia* would be most appropriate for this purpose because they are animals rather than plants. Scientists in government or industry might use *Daphnia,* along with other invertebrates and fish, to address this herbicide toxicity question.

CONCENTRATION VERSUS DOSE

If you want to measure the toxicity of a compound to *Daphnia*, fish, or other organisms that live in water, you are not likely to feed the compound to the organisms directly. Instead, you place the bioassay organisms in chemical solutions, then count how many individuals die within a given time period. In these aquatic dose/response experiments, the end result is the LC_{50}, the concentration that is lethal to 50% of the exposed organisms.

For aquatic bioassays in which the endpoint is something other than death, the results are expressed in terms of the TC_{50}, the concentration that causes 50% drop in growth or health of the test organisms.

In lettuce seed bioassays, for example, the seeds don't die—they either sprout and begin to grow or they remain unsprouted. So in this case you want to be able to express the amount of germination and growth rather than just survival. The TC_{50} represents the concentration at which the organisms in the treatment do approximately half as well as those in the control group.

LC_{50}s and TC_{50}s are expressed in terms of milligrams of chemical per liter of water (mg/L). These values are used to express the toxicity to aquatic organisms of known chemicals such as pesticides and water treatment compounds. They also are used to compare the toxicities of environmental samples such as discharges from factories or runoff from golf courses.

AN INTRODUCTION TO EXPERIMENTAL DESIGN

When you set up a dose/response bioassay, you will expose test organisms to solutions of various concentrations. Each of these concentrations is called a *treatment* in your experiment. The factor that you change is called the *independent variable*. In a dose/response experiment, the independent variable is the concentration of the test chemical. The *dependent variable* is the response that you expect to measure, such as the number of *Daphnia* that have died or of lettuce seeds that have sprouted.

In addition to the treatments, you will have an untreated group that will serve as your *control*. Organisms in the control group get exposed to all of the same conditions as those in the treatment groups, except that they are grown in water without any of the test chemical added. The control group serves as a standard of comparison so that you can see how well the organisms do when they are not exposed to your test chemical.

An ***LC50*** is the concentration that kills 50% of the test organisms.

A ***TC50*** is the concentration that causes a 50% drop in growth or health of the test organisms.

The ***treatments*** in an experiment represent the factor that you vary while keeping everything else constant.

The ***control*** is the untreated group, used for comparison with the treatment groups.

Replicates are groups of organisms exposed to identical conditions.

Within each of your treatments, you will have more than one set of organisms. For example, in the lettuce seed bioassay, you will set up several petri dishes for each chemical concentration. These are called *replicates*, and they are exposed to exactly the same experimental conditions. Each beaker containing *Daphnia* is one replicate for that particular concentration of the test solution. In a duckweed bioassay, each beaker containing plants and test solution is one replicate.

The more replicates you can manage, the better, but you will have to figure out how many are possible with the supplies and time you have available. Can you think of a reason why it is better to have replicates rather than just adding more individuals to each petri dish or beaker? For example, what if one of the dishes got contaminated—which of these approaches would give you more useful results?

Another decision you will need to make in designing a bioassay experiment is what conditions to keep constant among all the treatments. Examples include the temperature, the exposure time, the exposure to sunlight, and the number of organisms used.

INTERPRETING BIOASSAY RESULTS

In any sort of bioassay, the hardest steps are interpreting the results and deciding what types of conclusions are valid. For example, in dose/response experiments using laboratory rats, it is relatively simple to determine the LD_{50} but much trickier to figure out what this might mean in terms of toxicity to humans. Similarly, in dose/response experiments using *Daphnia*, it is important to carefully consider how to interpret the LC_{50} values. What conclusions are valid about possible environmental impacts of the compounds tested?

In general, dose/response bioassays are useful in comparing the toxicity of various compounds. For example, calcium chloride and magnesium chloride are sometimes described as "environmentally friendly" alternatives to sodium chloride for melting ice on sidewalks and roads. After carrying out bioassays on these compounds, you could conclude which is least toxic to the types of organism you used.

For environmental testing, bioassays provide a means of comparing the toxicity of samples from different locations or times. For example, you might be able to conclude that stream sediment downstream from your school parking lot is 10 times more toxic to duckweed than sediment from upstream sites. Or your bioassays might show that the parking lot runoff was far less toxic in April than in February.

It is important to remember that bioassays do not specify what chemicals are present in environmental samples. Instead, they provide a measure of the combined toxicity of whatever is in the sample. Environmental bioassays provide a standardized technique for comparing the toxicities of environmental samples taken at various sites or times. They also can be used to compare the toxicities of environmental samples to those of known chemical solutions.

The following sections of this book provide instructions for carrying out bioassays and designing your own toxicology experiments. Once you learn the basic techniques, you will be able to use bioassays to investigate a wide range of questions concerning the toxicity of chemical solutions and environmental samples.

Have fun, and good luck!

Some Tips for Planning an Experiment
http://ei.cornell.edu/student/exptdesign.asp

FOR DISCUSSION

▶ Why are *Daphnia* and duckweed more appropriate test organisms than laboratory mice for environmental bioassays?

▶ Why are lettuce seeds useful for environmental bioassays even though they would not naturally be found in habitats such as ponds or streams?

▶ What information would you expect to get from bioassays that you would not be able to get from chemical measurements?

REFERENCES

Andress, E.L. 1991. *Botulism: It Only Takes a Taste.* Fact Sheet HE-8198. Gainesville, Fla: University of Florida, Institute of Food and Agricultural Sciences.

Carson, R. 1962. *Silent Spring.* Boston: Houghton Mifflin.

TOXICOLOGY PROTOCOLS:
INTRODUCTION TO RESEARCH

TOXICOLOGY PROTOCOLS

PROTOCOL 1. SERIAL DILUTIONS

Objective

To make a serial dilution for use in dose/response bioassays.

Background

The idea behind a bioassay is that the test organism will respond in a predictable way to varying concentrations of a chemical compound. You can test this idea using dose/response experiments (Protocols 2, 3, and 4). For example, if you place *Daphnia* in a beaker containing a concentrated salt solution, they will all quickly die. In a beaker containing water with no salt, most of the *Daphnia* should remain alive and healthy during the two-day test period. At intermediate salt concentrations, the number of surviving individuals and the length of time they survive should vary depending on the solution concentrations.

The first step in carrying out a dose/response experiment is to create a wide range of concentrations of your test solution. Initially, you probably will have no idea what concentrations will kill your test organisms and what concentrations will cause them no harm. Therefore, it is a good idea to start by testing a very wide range of concentrations. You can do this by creating a serial dilution—a series of solutions, each of which is ten times more dilute than the one from which it is made.

As you can see, each solution is ten times less concentrated than the one just above it in Table 2.1. The solution in the bottom row of the table has a concentration measured in

TABLE 2.1
An Example Serial Dilution

Concentration	Percent Concentration
25 g/L = 25,000 mg/L = 25 parts per thousand	100%
2.5 g/L = 2,500 mg/L = 2.5 parts per thousand	10%
0.25 g/L = 250 mg/L = 250 parts per million	1%
0.025 g/L = 25 mg/L = 25 parts per million	0.1%
0.0025 g/L = 2.5 mg/L = 2.5 parts per million	0.01%
0.00025 g/L = 0.25 mg/L = 250 parts per billion	0.001%

terms of parts per billion (ppb). This may seem inconceivably small and impossible to measure, but in fact biological organisms are sensitive to many different chemicals in concentrations as low as parts per billion. Many drinking water standards are measured in this range. For example, the drinking water standard for lead is 15 ppb, meaning that public water suppliers must take action if concentrations higher than this are measured in their drinking water supplies.

You may be wondering what "100% concentration" means. It simply means the highest concentration in your dilution series. It can be whatever concentration you choose—just remember to write down what chemical you are using and what concentration (in mg/L) you have selected to be the 100% concentration (see Step 1).

Materials (per student group)

▶ Balance

▶ 6 × 250 mL beakers, flasks, or cups

▶ 1 × 100 mL graduated cylinder

▶ 1 × 10 mL pipette or graduated cylinder

▶ Pipette bulb (if using pipettes)

▶ Tape or wax pencil for labeling flasks

▶ Parafilm or plastic wrap

▶ Test chemical (consult with your teacher)

▶ Goggles

▶ 2 L spring water*

*Note: Distilled water can be used if the serial dilution solutions will be used with lettuce seed bioassays. For bioassays using duckweed or *Daphnia*, solutions should be made using unchlorinated water such as bottled spring water because distilled water will not adequately support the growth of these organisms (see **Culture Water** in *Teacher's Guide*, p. 46).

Procedure

1. Label the six beakers with your name, the date, and the percent concentrations listed in Table 2.1, adding the name or chemical formula for your test chemical. For example, your label might read "NaCl 100%". Make sure to record the concentration of your 100% solution:

    100% solution = _____ mg/L of _____
    chemical name

2. Consult your teacher to determine the specified weight of your test chemical. Weigh out this amount and place it in the beaker labeled "100%". Add 100 mL water and swirl gently until the crystals are fully dissolved.

3. Using a 10 mL pipette or graduated cylinder, transfer 10 mL of your 100% solution to the beaker labeled "10%". Add 90 mL water and swirl gently to mix. ***Caution: Never pipette by mouth! Instead, be sure to use a pipette bulb or a syringe-style pipette to avoid accidentally getting a mouthful of your chemical solution.***

4. After thoroughly rinsing the 10 mL pipette, transfer 10 mL of your 10% solution to the beaker labeled "1%", then add 90 mL water and swirl to mix.

5. Continue with this dilution process until you have made all five dilutions. Unless you will be using the solutions right away, cover them tightly with plastic wrap to prevent water loss through evaporation.

PROTOCOL 2. DOSE/RESPONSE EXPERIMENTS USING LETTUCE SEEDS

Objective

To conduct a dose/response bioassay using lettuce seeds.

Background

A bioassay is an experiment that uses living things to test the toxicity of chemicals. One kind of bioassay is a dose/response experiment, in which you expose the test organisms to various doses of a chemical and then measure their responses. In this protocol, lettuce seeds are the test organisms. After placing lettuce seeds in dishes containing various concentrations of a chemical, you count how many seeds have sprouted and then measure the lengths of the roots that have grown.

For example, if you place lettuce seeds in petri dishes containing a concentrated copper sulfate solution, none of the seeds will sprout. If you place seeds in dishes containing distilled water, most of them should germinate and grow. At concentrations in between, the number of seeds that sprout and the length of their roots should vary depending on the concentrations of the solutions.

In this protocol, you will carry out a dose/response experiment to test the sensitivity of lettuce seeds to the serial dilutions you created in Protocol 1.

Materials (per student group)

▶ 105 lettuce seeds (Buttercrunch is the standard variety. Others will work, but be sure to use only one variety and record its name.)

▶ 21 × 100 mm petri dishes and plastic bag(s) to hold them

▶ 21 round paper filters (7.5 or 9 cm diameter)

▶ 50 mL 10% bleach solution (5 mL bleach in 45 mL water)

▶ Tape or wax pencil for labeling petri dishes

▶ Metric rulers graduated in mm

▶ Tweezers

▶ One 2 mL or 5 mL pipette

▶ Pipette bulb (unless using syringe-style transfer pipettes)

▶ Funnel and coffee filters (for rinsing seeds)

▶ 6 mL of each of the chemical solutions made in Protocol 1

▶ 500 mL distilled water (for rinsing)

▶ 6 mL distilled water or spring water from source used in Protocol 1

Procedure

1. Soak the lettuce seeds in a 10% bleach solution for five minutes. Strain through a coffee filter and rinse thoroughly. This kills bacteria and fungi that can interfere with seed germination.

2. In each of 21 100 mm petri dishes place a paper filter. Label three dishes with your name, the date, and the name and concentration of each of the solutions you made in Protocol 1. Label the final three dishes "control."

3. To each petri dish, add 2 mL of the appropriate test solution. Thoroughly rinse the pipette between solutions. *Caution: Never pipette by mouth! Instead, be sure to use a pipette bulb or a syringe-style pipette to avoid accidentally getting a mouthful of your chemical solution.*

4. In the control dishes, use distilled or spring water as your test solution, depending on which type of water you used to make your serial dilutions in Protocol 1.

5. To each dish, add five pretreated lettuce seeds, spaced evenly on the filter paper so that they do not touch each other or the sides of the dish.

6. Place the dishes in a plastic bag and seal it to retain moisture. Incubate the seeds in the dark for five days, preferably at a constant temperature of 24.5° C.

7. At the end of the five-day growth period, count and record how many seeds in each dish have germinated. For each sprout, measure the radicle length to the nearest mm. *(The radicle is the embryonic root.)* Look carefully at the plants to make sure you are measuring just the radicle, not the shoot as well. For example, in the picture below, you would measure just the part between the two arrows, not the rest of the sprout to the left. Enter your data in Tables 2.2a and 2.2b.

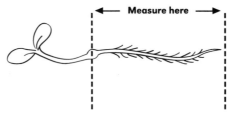

8. Graph the mean (average) for each treatment using Figures 2.2a and 2.2b. Then analyze your data using the guidelines below.

Analysis—How Good Are Your Data?

Once you have counted how many seeds sprouted and measured their radicle lengths, then what? How can you interpret these results?

Comparison to the Control

The first thing to check is your control (the dishes that contain water rather than a chemical solution). The purpose of the control is to identify how well the seeds will grow without any added chemicals. Would you expect all the seeds in your control dishes to germinate? Probably not, just as a gardener does not expect all the seeds in a garden to sprout.

If fewer than 80% of the seeds in your control dishes sprouted, something may have gone wrong in your experiment. Perhaps the seeds were too old or stored improperly, so they are no longer viable. You can test whether your seeds are in good condition using a technique popular among gardeners—simply roll a few seeds in a damp paper towel, seal it in a plastic bag, and then check the germination rate after a few days.

Another possible problem is that something went wrong with the conditions for growth. Did the dishes get too hot, too dry, or contaminated in some way?

Analysis of Trends

Looking at your graphs of average number of seeds germinated and average radicle lengths (Figures 2.2a and 2.2b), do you notice any trends? For example, does the toxicity of your test chemical appear to increase as the concentration increases, or does it stay the same from one concentration to the next? Are there any data that don't seem to make sense? If so, make a note of these and try to think of any possible explanations for why they are different from your expectations.

A Look at Variability

The means for each treatment tell only part of the story. It is also useful to take a look at the individual data points to see how much variability exists within each treatment. In the case of lettuce seed bioassays, this means looking at the number of seeds sprouted per dish and the lengths of their radicles. Did the replicate dishes show similar numbers of seeds sprouting, and similar average radicle lengths? In bioassays, variability is inevitable because of the biological differences among organisms. Within the control group, for example, it is common to find some seeds that do not germinate, others that grow radicles only a few millimeters long, and others that reach 10 times this length.

Try graphing individual data points for each treatment. The wider the spread between data points, the greater the variability within that treatment. The more variability there is within each treatment, the less confident you can be that one treatment is different from another, even if the averages appear different on your bar graph (Figure 2.2a or 2.2b).

In addition to the inevitable variability caused by biological differences among organisms, your experimental techniques also will influence the variability of your data. At many steps in a bioassay, the measurements and decisions you make will affect your results. Were the serial dilutions carefully made according to directions? Were precise amounts of solution put into each petri dish? Did one person measure radicle lengths, or did two or more people share this task? Did you stretch some radicles more than others while measuring them, or did you treat them all the same? Based on your experience with this bioassay protocol, what ideas do you have for reducing variability caused by measurement techniques?

Estimating the TC$_{50}$

The next step in your data analysis is to figure out how to answer the question:

How toxic is the solution or sample to the type of organism you tested?

In bioassays there are two ways to report results: LC$_{50}$, the lethal concentration that kills 50% of the test organisms, and TC$_{50}$, the toxic concentration that causes organisms to grow 50% as well as the control group. In lettuce seed bioassays, the seeds don't die—they either sprout and begin to grow, or they remain unsprouted. So, in this case use the TC$_{50}$ to represent the concentration at which the lettuce seeds in the treatment grow approximately half as well as those in the control group. (See Section 1, Chapter 4 for further explanation of TC$_{50}$.)

For lettuce seed bioassays, there are two possible TC$_{50}$s—one for germination rate and another for radicle length. Using Figures 2.2a and 2.2b, you can estimate which concentrations produce germination and growth rates roughly half those of the control group. If none of your concentrations produces rates that are close to half those of the control, it makes sense to report the TC50 as a range rather than a single number. For example:

The TC50 for lettuce seed germination must be higher than all the concentrations I tested because more than half of the seeds sprouted in all my test solutions.

or

In this experiment, the TC50 for lettuce seed radicle length lies somewhere between 50 and 500 mg/L. I would need to conduct another bioassay of concentrations within this range to specify the TC50 more precisely.

Drawing Conclusions about Toxicity

After you have estimated the TC50 for your experiment, you will be able to use this number to make a statement about the toxicity of the substance you tested. Usually this statement will be something like:

The TC50 for chemical X and lettuce seed radicle length is in the range of __ to __.

If you have TC50 values for lettuce seeds exposed to other chemicals, you can use these numbers to rank which chemicals are most toxic to lettuce seeds. For example:

The TC50 for chemical X is a smaller number than the TC50 for chemical Y. This means that chemical X can affect lettuce seed radicle growth at lower concentrations than chemical Y. Therefore, I conclude that chemical X is more toxic to lettuce growth than chemical Y.

It is important to remember that lettuce seed bioassays will not help you to reach conclusions about toxicity to humans because humans and lettuce are likely to respond very differently to chemical exposures. In order to use bioassays to predict toxicity to humans, you would need to use organisms such as laboratory rats that are known to provide a better model of human response to toxic chemicals.

LETTUCE SEED DOSE/RESPONSE BIOASSAY DATA SHEET

Name_____ Date_____

Chemical tested   _____

100% concentration _____ mg/L

Length of experiment _____ days

Constants (such as temperature and light) _____

TABLE 2.2a
Seed Germination Data

Concentration (%)	Concentration (mg/L)	# Seeds Germinated/Dish			Average # Seeds Germinated
Control					
0.001%					
0.01%					
0.1%					
1%					
10%					
100%					

TABLE 2.2b
Radicle Length Data

Concentration (%)	Radicle Length (mm)												Average Length (mm)
Control													
0.001%													
0.01%													
0.1%													
1%													
10%													
100%													

FIGURE 2.2a
Lettuce Seed Germination

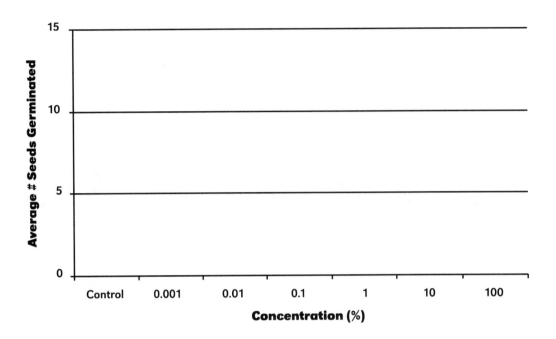

FIGURE 2.2b
Lettuce Seed Radicle Length

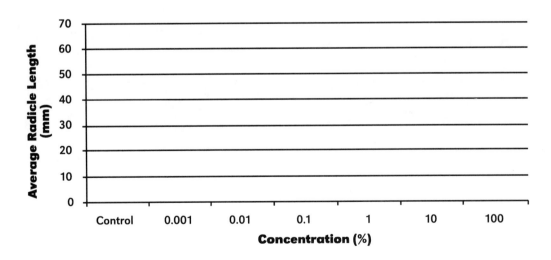

Name_____ Date_____

Some questions to consider: *(Please use full sentences.)*

1. Did at least 80% of the seeds in the control dishes germinate? If not, what would you recommend doing differently next time to try to get a better germination rate?

2. Did lettuce seed germination respond in a predictable way to concentration? Describe any trends you observed.

3. Do any of your data not fit the trends you observed? If so, can you think of any reasons why these data might lie outside the range you would expect?

4. What is your estimate of the TC50 based on your lettuce seed germination data?

$$TC_{50} = \_\_\_\_$$

    What is your estimate of the TC50 based on your radicle length data?

$$TC_{50} = \_\_\_\_$$

    Which shows a greater response to the chemical you tested: germination rate or radicle length? Describe any similarities or differences that you noticed in trends between these two indicators of toxicity.

5. What can you conclude about the toxicity of the substance you tested? Is this what you expected? Was your hypothesis supported by the data?

6. If other students carried out a dose/response experiment using the same chemical, did their data follow the same trends as yours?

7. Based on this experiment, would you say that lettuce seed germination or root length would provide a useful bioassay for water samples from the environment? Why or why not?

8. If you were going to repeat this experiment, what would you do differently? How might you improve the experimental design to reduce the variability of your data or lead to more reliable results?

PROTOCOL 3. DOSE/RESPONSE EXPERIMENTS USING DUCKWEED

Objective

To conduct a dose/response bioassay using duckweed.

Background

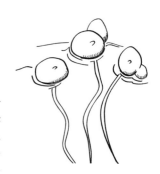

A bioassay is an experiment that uses living things to test the toxicity of chemicals. One kind of bioassay is a dose/response experiment in which you expose organisms to various doses of a chemical and then measure their responses. In this protocol, duckweed is used as the bioassay organism. After placing duckweed plants in beakers containing various concentrations of a chemical, you monitor their growth and health over a five-day period.

Duckweed is a small aquatic plant that floats on the surface of ponds, wetlands, and nutrient-rich lakes. Worldwide, there are over 40 species of duckweed (family Lemnaceae), with 20 species found in the United States. *Lemna minor* is the species most commonly used for bioassays. Each *Lemna* plant consists of one or more fronds. The fronds look like little leaves but actually are a combination of leaf and stem, attached to a rootlet that dangles down in the water.

Although duckweed is a flowering plant, it rarely flowers. Usually it reproduces through budding—new fronds grow from buds on the parent plant. Eventually these new fronds grow their own roots and break off to become independent plants. When you conduct a bioassay using duckweed, you measure growth rate by counting how many new fronds develop over a five-day growth period.

In this protocol, you will carry out a dose/response experiment to test the sensitivity of duckweed to the serial dilutions you created in Protocol 1.

Materials (per student group)

▶ Fluorescent or plant grow lights

▶ 105 duckweed plants

▶ 21 beakers or clear plastic cups

▶ Miracle-Gro Liquid Houseplant Food Drops
  or similar fertilizer solution (N:P:K = 8:7:6)

▶ Eye dropper (for fertilizer)

▶ Tweezers or paper clips (for handling duckweed)

▶ Clear plastic film such as Saran Wrap

▶ 90 mL of each of the chemical solutions made in Protocol 1

▶ 90 mL spring water from source used in Protocol 1

▶ 100 mL distilled water (for rinsing)

Procedure

1. Label beakers or cups with your name, the date, and the solution concentrations listed in Table 2.1 (p. 41). Label the final three beakers "control" (three beakers per concentration).

2. Pour 30 mL solution into each of the beakers, following the labels for solution concentrations. In the control beakers, use spring water instead of a chemical solution. Add one drop of liquid fertilizer to each beaker.

3. Using tweezers or an unfolded paper clip, gently transfer five duckweed plants into each beaker. (Avoid using your fingers because that could introduce other chemicals into your culture solutions.) Choose only green, healthy-looking plants that have two fronds apiece and are approximately the same size.

4. Cover the beakers with clear plastic film, and place them under 24-hour fluorescent or plant grow lights. (Artificial lighting is optimal because it provides consistent conditions from one experiment to another. Indirect natural lighting is an acceptable alternative. Avoid placing the beakers directly in a sunny window because overheating may cause the duckweeds to get scorched.)

5. Let the beakers sit undisturbed for five days. Keep them covered with plastic, and do not add water to them during this time.

6. At the end of the five-day growth period, count the number of fronds in each beaker. It may be difficult to decide which fronds are real, and which are too small to count. The important thing is to be consistent so that your results will be comparable across treatments.

7. Record your data in Table 2.3 and make notes about any plants that are yellow, rootless, or sinking, or that otherwise appear unhealthy.

8. Using Figure 2.3, graph the mean (average) for each treatment. Then analyze your data using the guidelines below.

Analysis

Comparison to the Control

The first thing to check is your control (the beakers that contain just spring water and fertilizer solution). The purpose of the control is to identify how well the duckweed will grow under uncontaminated conditions.

You can expect the number of fronds to roughly double in the control beakers during the five-day incubation period. If your control plants did not grow much or do not look healthy, something may have gone wrong in your experiment. Perhaps the nutrient solution was too strong or too weak, or the plants were not healthy to begin with. Or maybe a problem developed with the environmental conditions. Did the solutions get too hot, too dry, or contaminated in some way?

Analysis of Trends

Looking at your graph (Figure 2.3), do you notice any trends? For example, does the toxicity of your test chemical appear to increase as the concentration increases, or does it stay the same from one concentration to the next? Are there any data that don't seem to make sense?

If so, make a note of these and try to think of any possible explanations for why they are different from your expectations.

A Look at Variability

The means for each treatment tell only part of the story. It is also useful to take a look at the individual data points (the number of fronds in each of the three beakers) to get an idea how much variability exists within each treatment. Try graphing individual data points for each treatment. The wider the spread between data points, the greater the variability within that treatment. The more variability there is within each treatment, the less confident you can be that one treatment is different from another, even if the means appear different on your bar graph (Figure 2.3).

Because of individual differences among organisms, you shouldn't expect each plant to respond in exactly the same way. However, it is reasonable to expect that the groups of individuals in each treatment will follow predictable trends. Did replicate beakers have similar numbers of duckweed fronds at the end of the five-day growth period? If your data are more variable than you think is reasonable, you could look into the potential sources of this variability. For example, did the plants appear to be healthy at the beginning of your experiment, or were they already stressed? Were the serial dilutions carefully made according to directions? Did one person do all the counting of duckweed fronds, or did two or more people share this task? Based on your experience with this bioassay protocol, what ideas do you have for reducing variability caused by measurement techniques?

Estimating the TC50

The next step in your data analysis is to figure out how to answer the question:

How toxic is the solution or sample to the type of organism you tested?

In bioassays there are two ways to report results: LC50, the lethal concentration that kills 50% of the test organisms, and TC50, the toxic concentration that causes organisms to grow 50% as well as a control group. In duckweed bioassays, the plants don't necessarily die—they may just grow more slowly than they would in a less toxic solution. So in this case use the TC50 to represent the concentration at which the duckweed in the treatment grow approximately half as well as those in the control group.

Using Figure 2.3, you can estimate at what concentration the duckweed has grown roughly half as much as the plants in the control group. If none of your concentrations produce rates that are close to half those of the control, it makes sense to report the TC50 as a range rather than a single number. For example, you might have to say that the TC50 is greater than or less than all the concentrations you tested, or that it lies somewhere between two of your tested concentrations.

Drawing Conclusions about Toxicity

After you have estimated the TC50 for your experiment, you will be able to use this number to make a statement about the toxicity of the substance you were testing. Usually this statement will be something like:

The TC50 for chemical X and duckweed growth is in the range of __ to __.

If you have TC50 values for duckweed exposed to other chemicals, you can use these numbers to rank which chemicals are most toxic to duckweed. For example:

The TC50 for chemical X is a smaller number than the TC50 for chemical Y. This means that chemical X can affect duckweed growth at lower concentrations than chemical Y. Therefore, I conclude that chemical X is more toxic to duckweed growth than chemical Y.

It is important to remember that duckweed bioassays are not designed to help you reach conclusions about toxicity to humans because duckweed plants and humans are likely to respond very differently to chemical exposures. In order to use bioassays to predict toxicity to humans, you would need to use organisms such as laboratory rats that are known to provide a better model of human response to toxic chemicals.

DUCKWEED DOSE/RESPONSE BIOASSAY DATA SHEET

Name_____ Date_____

Chemical tested   _____

100% concentration _____ mg/L

Length of experiment _____ days

Constants (such as temperature and light) _____

TABLE 2.3
Duckweed Bioassay Data

Solution Concentration	# Duckweed Fronds/Beaker			Avg. # Fronds	Comments about Plant Health
Control					
0.001%					
0.01%					
0.1%					
1%					
10%					
100%					

FIGURE 2.3
Duckweed Bioassay Results

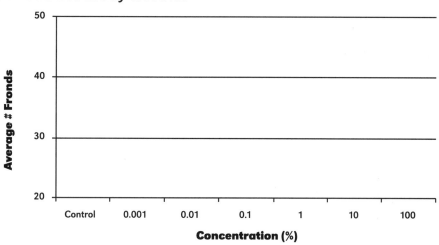

Name_____ Date_____

Some questions to consider: *(Please use full sentences.)*

1. Did the duckweed colonies grow well in the control beakers? Do your control plants appear healthy? If not, what would you recommend trying differently for the next round of experiments?

2. Did duckweed growth respond in a predictable way to concentration? Describe any trends you observed.

3. Do any of your data not fit the trends you observed? If so, can you think of any reasons why these data might lie outside the range you would expect?

4. What TC_{50} would you estimate based on your duckweed data?

$$TC_{50} = \text{\_\_\_\_}$$

If it is impossible to estimate the TC_{50} from your data, please explain why.

5. What can you conclude about the toxicity of the substance you tested? Is this what you expected? Was your hypothesis supported by the data?

6. If other students carried out a dose/response experiment using the same chemical, did their data follow the same trends as yours?

7. Based on this experiment, would you say that duckweed would be a useful bioassay organism for water samples from the environment? Why or why not?

8. If you were going to repeat this experiment, what would you do differently? How might you improve the experimental design to reduce the variability of your data or lead to more reliable results?

PROTOCOL 4. DOSE/RESPONSE EXPERIMENTS USING *DAPHNIA*

Objective

To conduct a dose/response bioassay using *Daphnia*.

Background

A bioassay is an experiment that uses living things to test the toxicity of chemicals. One kind of bioassay is a dose/response experiment in which you expose the test organisms to various doses of a chemical and then measure their responses. In this protocol, *Daphnia* are the test organisms. *Daphnia* are tiny crustaceans that look like fleas as they hop around in water. They are related to lobsters and crabs, but live in fresh water such as ponds, lakes, and slow-moving streams.

To use *Daphnia* in dose/response bioassays, you place them in beakers containing various concentrations of a chemical, then count how many die over a two-day period. If they all die, then you can try again with lower chemical concentrations. Ideally, you will find a range of concentrations in which most of the *Daphnia* die at the highest concentrations, and most of them survive at the lowest concentrations.

Materials (per student group)

▶ 22 beakers or transparent cups

▶ 1 × 20 mL graduated cylinder

▶ 1 pipette with 5 mm diameter opening
(a disposable plastic pipette with the tip trimmed off works well)

▶ *Daphnia magna* culture (at least 105 individuals)

▶ 100 mL of distilled water (for rinsing)

▶ 60 mL of each of the chemical solutions made in Protocol 1

▶ 60 mL spring water from source used in Protocol 1

Procedure

1. Prior to starting the bioassay, check the *Daphnia* to ensure the culture is healthy. Most of the individuals should be hopping around in the water, not lying motionless or doing somersaults at the bottom of the culture container.

2. Using a pipette with a 5 mm tip, collect small, young *Daphnia* from your cultures and transfer them into a beaker, pouring off extra water to make a concentrated collection of organisms for use in your bioassay. Be sure to collect only *Daphnia* that are small and don't contain visible eggs or young in their brood chamber (see Figure 3.5 p. 87)

3. Label three beakers or cups with each of the solution concentrations listed in Table 2.1 (Protocol 1), and fill each container with 20 mL of the appropriate solution. The final three beakers should be labeled "control" and filled with 20 mL spring water.

4. Transfer five *Daphnia* into each beaker, being careful to minimize the amount of culture water you add to the test solutions. Be sure to release the young below the surface of each

solution to avoid exposing them to the air. Rinse the pipette between solutions to avoid cross-contamination.

5. Using Table 2.4, record the total number of *Daphnia* that are dead at each time interval for each concentration. Table 2.4 lists 1 hour, 24 hours, and 48 hours as the time intervals, but you can change this if your schedule requires different timing. As close to one hour as possible, but before the end of the period, record the number dead at each concentration. It may be confusing because *Daphnia* shed their shells as they grow, and these shells can look like dead organisms. Therefore, you may find it easier to count the number of surviving *Daphnia* and use that number to figure out how many have died.

6. Using Figure 2.4, graph the mean (average) number of *Daphnia* that have died after 24 hours in each treatment. Then analyze your data using the guidelines below.

Analysis

Comparison to the Control

First, take a look at your control group. These individuals were not exposed to your test chemical, and you might have expected all of them to survive. If a few died, that's OK—with any type of living organism there is variability in health, life span, and sensitivity to environmental conditions. But if 20% or more of the *Daphnia* in your control group died, you should take a look at the test conditions. Perhaps the water got too hot on a sunny windowsill, or the individuals you started out with were not young and healthy. You might want to take a look at the optimal conditions listed in the *Teacher's Guide,* p. 47 and try the experiment again.

If fewer than 20% of the control group died (<3 of the 15 individuals you started with), then you can go on to analyze the data for your treatments.

Analysis of Trends

Looking at your graph (Figure 2.4), do you notice any trends? For example, does the toxicity of your test chemical appear to increase as the concentration increases, or does it stay the same from one concentration to the next? Are there any data that don't seem to make sense? If so, make a note of these and try to think of any possible explanations for why they are different from your expectations.

A Look at Variability

The means for each treatment tell only part of the story. It is also useful to take a look at the individual data points (# *Daphnia* dead in each of the three beakers) to get an idea how much variability exists within each treatment. Try graphing individual data points for each treatment. The wider the spread between data points, the greater the variability within that treatment. The more variability there is within each treatment, the less confident you can be that one treatment is different from another, even if the means appear different on your bar graph.

Within each treatment, how much variability did you find in your results? Did replicate beakers have similar numbers of *Daphnia* surviving? If you think the data are much more variable than you would expect, you might want to explore the potential sources of variability. For example, can you remember having had any problem in finding enough young and healthy-looking *Daphnia* to add to each solution? Were you able to add the same number of

Daphnia to each solution, without adding a lot of extra water? Were all of the beakers kept under identical conditions during the bioassay, or did some get hotter or exposed to brighter light? What ideas can you come up with for reducing the variability in your results if you were to run this experiment again?

Estimating the LC50

The next step in your data analysis is to figure out how to answer the question:

How toxic is the solution or sample to the type of organism you tested?

Bioassays are designed to estimate the concentration of a test material that affects 50% of the test organisms. The concentration that kills half of the test animals over a specified period of time is called the LC50 (this stands for lethal concentration for 50% of the test population). From your graph in Figure 2.4, make an estimate of the LC50 for the chemical you tested.

It may be necessary to report the LC50 as a range rather than a single number. For example, you might have to say that the LC50 is greater than or less than the concentrations you tested, or that it lies somewhere between two of your tested concentrations.

Drawing Conclusions about Toxicity

After you have estimated the LC50 for your experiment, you will be able to use this number to make a statement about the toxicity of the substance you were testing. Usually this statement will be something like:

The LC50 for chemical X and Daphnia *is in the range of __ to __.*

If you have LC50 values for *Daphnia* exposed to other chemicals, you can use these numbers to rank which chemicals are most toxic to *Daphnia*. For example:

The LC50 for chemical X is a smaller number than the LC50 for chemical Y. This means that chemical X can kill Daphnia *at lower concentrations than chemical Y. Therefore, I conclude that chemical X is more toxic to* Daphnia *than chemical Y.*

Bioassays using *Daphnia* cannot be translated directly into conclusions about toxicity to humans because humans and *Daphnia* are likely to respond very differently to chemical exposures. In order to use bioassays to predict toxicity to humans, you would need to use organisms such as laboratory rats that are known to provide a better model of human response to toxic chemicals.

DAPHNIA DOSE/RESPONSE BIOASSAY DATA SHEET

Name_____ Date_____

Chemical tested   _____

100% concentration   _____ mg/L

Length of experiment _____ days

Constants (such as temperature and light) _____

TABLE 2.4
Daphnia Bioassay Results

Concen-tration (%)	Concen-tration (mg/L)	# Dead after 1 hour	# Dead after 24 hours	# Dead after 48 hours	Average # Dead after 48 hours
Control					
0.001%					
0.01%					
0.1%					
1%					
10%					
100%					

FIGURE 2.4
Daphnia Bioassay Results

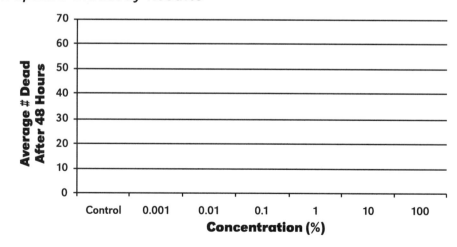

Name_____ Date_____

Some questions to consider: *(Please use full sentences.)*

1. **Did at least 80% of the *Daphnia* in the control beakers survive? If not, what would you recommend doing differently next time to try to get a better survival rate?**

2. **Did the rate of *Daphnia* survival respond in a predictable way to concentration? Describe any trends you observed.**

3. **Do any of your data not fit the trends you observed? If so, can you think of any reasons why these data might lie outside the range you would expect?**

4. **What LC50 would you estimate for your experiment with *Daphnia*?**

   LC50 = ____

   If it is impossible to estimate the LC50 from your data, please explain why.

5. What can you conclude about the toxicity of the substance you tested? Is this what you expected? Was your hypothesis supported by the data?

6. Think about whether any of the *Daphnia* might have died for reasons other than poisoning by the chemical you tested. What other factors do you think might possibly have killed some of them?

7. If other students carried out a dose/response experiment using the same chemical, did their data follow the same trends as yours?

8. Based on this experiment, would you say *Daphnia* would provide a useful bioassay organism for water samples from the environment? Why or why not?

9. If you were going to repeat this experiment, what would you do differently? How might you improve the experimental design to reduce the variability of your data or lead to more reliable results?

PROTOCOL 5. TESTING ENVIRONMENTAL SAMPLES USING BIOASSAYS

Objective

To test the toxicity of environmental samples using lettuce seed, duckweed, and/or *Daphnia* bioassays.

Background

Using dose/response experiments (Protocols 2–4), you can determine the sensitivity of bioassay organisms to specific chemical compounds. Another use of bioassays is quite different—by exposing bioassay organisms to environmental samples, you can assess the combined toxicity of all the chemicals in these samples. Scientists in government and industry use bioassays to evaluate and regulate contamination, such as determining the most highly contaminated areas at a hazardous waste site or assessing the toxicity of wastewater before it is discharged into the environment.

You might choose to test a local stream, comparing water from several different sites. You also could test the stream or lake sediments, where heavy metals and some other types of pollution are likely to concentrate. Another possibility is to target a suspected pollution source, such as the drainage from the parking lot at your school, bus garage, or a nearby mall.

Materials

See Protocols 2, 3, and/or 4.

Procedure

Bioassay procedures for environmental samples are the same as those used in the dose/ response experiments except that water or sediment samples are used in place of known chemical solutions. Your 100% concentration will now be an environmental sample that has not been diluted.

Remember to include a control group so you will have a check on the health of your organisms and the growth conditions provided in your experiment. For lettuce seed bioassays, distilled water provides a good control. For bioassays using duckweed or *Daphnia*, use unchlorinated water such as bottled spring water for the control because distilled water will not adequately support the growth of these organisms. (See *Teacher's Guide,* p. 46 for further information.) For duckweed bioassays, add fertilizer solution as described in Protocol 3.

If you are testing solids such as stream sediments or parking lot dirt, you will have to slightly modify the bioassay techniques:

▶ For lettuce seed bioassays, place 3 g of sediment or soil samples in the bottom of each petri dish and cover with filter paper. If the sample does not contain enough moisture to saturate the filter paper, add up to 2 mL water as needed.

▶ For duckweed and *Daphnia* bioassays, shake 10 g of sample in 100 mL water, and then either filter or let the solids settle out before using the liquid for your bioassay experiments.

Ideally, the control for soil or sediment bioassays should be a soil or sediment sample that is similar in composition but taken from a location believed to be uncontaminated.

However, it is impossible to guarantee that any particular sample will be uncontaminated. We therefore recommend that you also set up a control with no soil (using just distilled or spring water) to provide an additional check on your experimental conditions.

Analysis

Just like in dose/response experiments, you should start your data analysis by checking the control group. In this case, the controls are the organisms that grew in water rather than in your environmental samples. Did the control organisms survive and grow as well as expected? (Check the *Comparison to the Control* section in Protocols 2–4 for guidelines about how the control organisms are expected to respond.)

After checking the control group, the next step is to summarize your data and look for trends. It is useful to calculate the mean for each sample and make graphs showing averages and individual data points. Then you can estimate the LC_{50} or TC_{50} just as you would in dose/response bioassays. (For further information, refer to the **Analysis** section in Protocols 2–4.)

There are three types of conclusions you may be able to make from your experiment:

1. *Conclusions about the toxicity of your samples.* You can use your LC_{50} or TC_{50} values to compare the toxicities of samples from various sources or sampling dates. If you have used more than one type of bioassay organism, you also can compare their responses to your samples. For example, you might say, "The parking lot runoff was more toxic to *Daphnia* than to duckweed at all of our sampling dates." Does this mean the water would also be toxic to humans? Not necessarily—to reach that conclusion, you would need to use bioassay organisms such as laboratory rats or mice that provide a better model of human toxicity.

   Remember, you will not be able to say what chemical is causing the toxicity based on your bioassay results—it could be one chemical or a combination of many, and it could be different chemicals from one sample to the next.

2. *Conclusions about the environment.* If very few of the organisms died in your environmental samples, you can conclude that the sources you tested are very low in toxicity to the test species. If many of the bioassay organisms died in your environmental samples but not in the control group, then you can conclude that there is something in the samples that is toxic to the test species.

   It is important to keep in mind that toxicity is just one piece of the puzzle determining environmental quality. If duckweed grows well in all of your stream samples, does this mean that the stream must be clean and pure? No, that would be too broad a conclusion. A more reasonable conclusion would be that the stream samples were nontoxic to duckweed. To reach a broader conclusion about the health of the stream, you would need to carry out chemical and biological surveys in addition to your bioassays.

3. *Recommendations about what to try next.* No matter how your experiment turns out, you can use your results in deciding what to try next. For example, if many of your control organisms died, you could recommend further tests to try to identify what went wrong. Were the beakers or the water contaminated? Were the organisms unhealthy to begin with? There are many possibilities that could be tested with further experiments. Remember, no experiment is a failure if you can learn from your results. Even if you got results that are totally different from what you expected, you can use these data to make recommendations for further research.

PROTOCOL 6. PREPARING WATER TREATMENT COLUMNS

Objective

To prepare ion exchange and activated charcoal columns for use in water treatment.

Background

An *ion* is an atom or group of atoms with an electrical charge. For example, when you stir a spoonful of salt into water, sodium chloride (NaCl) splits into two ions: sodium (Na^+) with a positive charge and chloride (Cl^-) with a negative charge. All natural sources of water contain many kinds of ions and molecules. Some of these chemicals are useful or at least harmless, but others need to be removed before the water is suitable for household or industrial uses. In this protocol, you will learn techniques for figuring out what classes of chemicals are in a solution and how they can potentially be removed.

One way of removing undesirable ions from a solution is by trickling it through a container filled with a special type of resin beads. This process is called *ion exchange* because ions originally attached to the resin trade places with other ions in the solution. You may be using ion exchange resins in your own home—in your water softener!

Water is called hard if it contains high concentrations of calcium (Ca^{+2}) and magnesium (Mg^{+2}) ions, or soft if it contains low concentrations of these ions. The calcium and magnesium ions in hard water present no problem to human health, but they can interfere with household and industrial water uses. Home water softeners are ion exchange columns containing beads of resin with attached sodium ions (Na^+). As hard water trickles past the resin beads, magnesium and calcium ions from the water get trapped, exchanging places with sodium ions that get released into solution. The end result is soft water, high in sodium but low in magnesium and calcium.

Water Softening Process

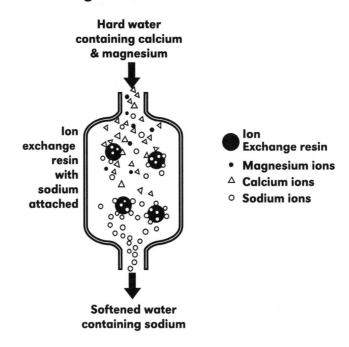

Hard water containing calcium & magnesium

Ion exchange resin with sodium attached

● Ion Exchange resin
• Magnesium ions
△ Calcium ions
○ Sodium ions

Softened water containing sodium

Water softening is an example of *cation* exchange. Cations are positively charged ions such as Ca^{+2}, Mg^{+2}, and Na^+. Other examples of cations include heavy metals such as cadmium (Cd^{+2}) and lead (Pb^{+2}), which are undesirable in drinking water because they can cause health problems in humans.

Using the same technique but a different type of resin, ion exchange can be used to remove undesirable *anions* from water. Anions are negatively charged ions such as nitrate (NO_3^-), which can cause "blue baby syndrome" in infants if the concentrations in drinking water are too high.

Not all chemicals are ions. Some are compounds with no electrical charge. Many pesticides and organic solvents are uncharged compounds, as are many of the natural substances that give a bad taste, odor, or color to water.

Uncharged compounds will not be removed from solution through ion exchange. Instead, another kind of treatment column is needed. In this case, the column is filled with a substance called activated charcoal. This is a powdered form of charcoal that has been treated at high temperature to increase its ability to remove chemicals from solution. Under the microscope, activated charcoal particles look like tiny sponges with many holes and pores that can trap and hold certain kinds of chemicals, including uncharged molecules.

You may be familiar with activated charcoal as an emergency treatment for poisoning. In this case, the charcoal works by trapping poisons in the stomach and preventing them from getting absorbed into the bloodstream. Aquarium filters also contain activated charcoal, as do many of the cartridge filters that people use to purify drinking water at home or when camping. Gas masks work on a similar principle, using activated charcoal to strip poisonous fumes from the air.

In this protocol, you will prepare three types of water treatment columns:

1. A cation exchange column for positively charged ions

2. An anion exchange column for negatively charged ions

3. An activated charcoal column for uncharged compounds

Each column consists of a tube filled with resin beads or activated charcoal.

Materials (per student group)

▶ 3 g strongly basic cation exchange resin (Dowex HCR-W2, Na^{+2} form, such as VWR #JT1928-1)

▶ 3 g strongly acidic anion exchange resin (IONAC A-554, Cl^- form, such as VWR #4605-1)

▶ 3 g activated charcoal (Darco G-60), washed with distilled water

▶ 3 small beakers or cups to hold the resin and/or activated charcoal

▶ Test tube rack, or ring stand with clamps (to hold treatment columns upright)

▶ 3 × 10 mL plastic syringes (without needles), such as Fisher #CVS30467-7*

▶ 100 mL distilled water

▶ Small amount of glass wool, soaked in distilled water

▶ Squirt bottle containing distilled water

▶ Piece of wire or thin tubing (for guiding the charcoal or resin into the syringes)

▶ Blunt stick (for tamping glass wool into syringe tips)

▶ 3 Hoffman screw-compressor clamps (½ × ¾"), such as Fisher #CVS49136

▶ Flexible tubing to attach to syringe tips, such as Fisher #CVS50615

*Note: These are used to make water treatment columns. If plastic syringes are not available, you can use beakers instead of building columns. Simply add the resin or charcoal to a small beaker containing each solution to be treated. Swirl for 10–15 minutes to bring the resin or charcoal into contact with the entire solution and then filter through a coffee filter to remove the solids from solution.

Procedure

1. Obtain three 10 mL syringes for use as water treatment columns. Each column will treat an 8 mL sample. If you want to treat a larger quantity of solution, you will need a larger column such as a burette to hold more resin.

2. Pack glass wool loosely into the tip of the column using a wooden stick or any blunt object. This plug of glass wool allows liquid to pass through but prevents resin or charcoal particles from leaking from the columns. Fill to about the 0.5 mL line with distilled water.

3. Fit a small piece of flexible tubing onto the tip of each column, and clamp the tubing closed. The Hoffman clamp allows you to regulate the flow of the effluent.

4. Place 3 g of cation exchange resin into a small beaker, add 10 mL distilled water, and gently swirl to wet the resin.

5. Fill the column with distilled water. Then unclamp the flexible tubing and allow the water to drain until it reaches the 1 mL mark in the column.

6. While swirling the beaker, carefully pour the resin-water mixture into the column. You may need a piece of wire or thin tubing to guide the slurry down the inside of the column. Once you begin filling the column, unclamp the tip of the tubing to allow the water to drip out at the rate of about 1 drop every 10 seconds. Using the clamp, adjust the flow whenever necessary.

7. Let the resin settle until it fills to about the 3 mL mark in the column, then close the clamp to keep the resin in the column covered with water.

8. Follow Steps 4–7 again, this time using anion exchange resin.

9. Prepare an activated charcoal column by following Steps 4–7 one more time. *Note:* the charcoal columns are filled to the 1 mL rather than 3 mL line because very little charcoal is needed for effective treatment of a sample, and too much charcoal will prevent the column from draining properly. If your column doesn't drain, simply unclamp the tip, turn the column upside down over a beaker, and squirt out some charcoal with distilled water. Fill the column with distilled water, let the charcoal settle, and regulate the flow rate to about 1 drop every 10 seconds.

10. Proceed to Protocol 7 for instructions on how to use these columns to remove toxic chemicals from water samples or chemical solutions.

PROTOCOL 7. CHEMICAL CLASSIFICATION OF TOXICANTS

Objective

To learn how water treatment columns can be used to remove toxic chemicals from water and to classify what types of compounds are causing the toxicity.

Background

In this protocol, we will use a solution of cupric chloride ($CuCl_2 \cdot 2H_2O$) as an example of a contaminant that contains ions that can be removed using the water treatment columns created in Protocol 6.

In water, cupric chloride separates into positive and negative ions: Cu^{+2} cations and Cl^- anions. By filtering the solution through the three kinds of treatment columns, you will be able to treat it with cation exchange, anion exchange, and activated charcoal. Then you will conduct a bioassay using the treated solutions to determine which column successfully reduces the toxicity of the solution.

We chose cupric chloride for this protocol because the solution starts out blue and becomes colorless as it passes through the cation exchange column. This makes a good visual example of ion exchange, but keep in mind that many other solutions can be detoxified using ion exchange or activated charcoal columns without undergoing any color change.

Materials (per student group)

▶ Water treatment columns prepared in Protocol 6

▶ 30 mL cupric chloride ($CuCl_2 \cdot 2H_2O$) solution (100 mg/L)

▶ Bioassay supplies (see Protocol 2, 3, or 4)

▶ 10 mL pipette

▶ Pipette bulb

▶ 50 mL beaker or cup

Procedure

1. Using columns prepared in Protocol 6, allow water to drain from each column until the water reaches just above the surface of the resin or charcoal.

2. Using a 10 mL pipette, slowly add 8 mL of 100 mg/L cupric chloride solution into each of your treatment columns.

3. Allow the columns to drip SLOWLY (about 1 drop per 10 seconds), collecting about 10 mL of the effluent into a small beaker. The effluent will be detoxified if it contains the right type of contaminant to be removed by the treatment column. Otherwise, it will remain untreated in spite of passing through the treatment column.

4. Set up a bioassay according to Protocol 2, 3, or 4 to test which of your columns has purified the cupric chloride solution. The following instructions use lettuce seed bioassays (Protocol 2) as an example, but similar experiments can be set up using duckweed (Protocol 3) or *Daphnia* (Protocol 4). The bioassay results will indicate whether any of

the columns have succeeded in removing toxic ions from solution. If the seeds exposed to the effluent sprout and grow well, you can conclude that that column successfully detoxified the solution. However, if seed germination and growth are inhibited compared with the control group, you can conclude that the treatment column did not successfully bind the toxic ions.

For a lettuce seed bioassay, set up 15 petri dishes and label them according to Table 2.5.

TABLE 2.5
Solutions for Cupric Chloride Bioassay

Sample #	Treatment
1 – 3	100 mg/L $CuCl_2 \cdot 2H_2O$
4 – 6	Effluent from anion exchange column
7 – 9	Effluent from cation exchange column
10 – 12	Effluent from activated charcoal column
13 – 15	Control

5. Soak the lettuce seeds in a 10% bleach solution for five minutes and then rinse thoroughly. This kills bacteria and fungi that can interfere with seed germination.

6. Place a paper filter in each of the 15 petri dishes and add 2 mL of the appropriate test solution. *Caution: Never pipette by mouth! Instead, be sure to use a pipette bulb or a syringe-style pipette to avoid accidentally getting a mouthful of your chemical solution.*

7. To each dish, add five pretreated lettuce seeds, spaced evenly on the filter paper so that they do not touch each other or the sides of the dish.

8. Place the dishes in a plastic bag and seal to retain moisture. Incubate the seeds in the dark for five days, preferably at a constant temperature of 24.5 °C.

9. At the end of the five-day growth period, count and record how many seeds in each dish have germinated. For each sprout, measure the radicle length to the nearest mm. *(The radicle is the embryonic root.)* Look carefully at the plants to make sure you are measuring just the radicle, not the shoot as well. For example, in the adjacent picture, you would measure just the part between the two arrows, not the rest of the sprout to the left. Enter your data in Tables 2.2a and 2.2b in Protocol 2.

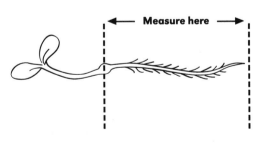

10. Graph and analyze your data using the guidelines in Protocol 2, and then answer the questions on the following **Data Interpretation** page.

BIOASSAYS TO TEST WATER TREATMENT
DATA INTERPRETATION

Name_____ Date_____

Chemical tested   _____

100% concentration   _____ mg/L

Some questions to consider: *(Please use full sentences.)*

1. What are we hoping to accomplish when we use water treatment columns before running a bioassay?

2. Based on your data for the untreated chemical solutions, would you say that this compound is toxic to lettuce seeds? Describe any trends you found in the average radicle length for the series of concentrations of untreated solutions.

3. Which (if any) of the three treatment columns removed a substance that is toxic to your bioassay organisms? How can you tell?

4. For the treatment column that worked best, what ions or compounds do you think are present in the solution after it has been treated? Draw an illustration showing what ions go into the top of the column and what ions you think are in the effluent that drains out the bottom.

5. Describe in your own words how this column purified the cupric chloride solution.

6. How do the radicle lengths of the seeds grown in effluent from this column compare to the control group?

7. What can you conclude—were you able to detoxify the sample by treating it with this column?

8. What can you conclude about the toxicity of cupric chloride? Does the Cu^{+2} cation, the Cl^- anion, or the whole compound cause the toxicity? What evidence leads you to reach this conclusion?

9. Briefly describe an experimental setup you could use to attempt to classify contaminants in an unknown such as water you have collected from a storm drain.

WORKSHEETS FOR PROTOCOLS

See Table 3 (p. 10 in *Teacher's Guide*) for a description of where each of these forms fits in the Environmental Inquiry (EI) process.

Additional worksheets are included in Protocols 2–4 for data analysis from dose/response experiments using lettuce seeds (pp. 47–50), duckweed (pp. 55–57), and *Daphnia* (pp. 61–63).

PROTOCOL PLANNING SHEET

Name_____ Date_____

1. What is the name of the protocol you will be using?

2. What is the purpose of this protocol?
   - ❑ Dose/response experiment
   - ❑ Bioassay on environmental samples
   - ❑ Solution purification using ion exchange and/or activated charcoal
   - ❑ Other _____

3. What question are you hoping to answer using this protocol?

4. What type of samples will you be testing?
   - ❑ Chemical name _____
   - ❑ Environmental samples from _____
   - ❑ Other _____

5. Describe the treatments you plan, such as the range of concentrations that you plan to test.

6. Describe your replicates of each treatment.

7. What will you be using for a control group?

8. What factors will you hold constant?

DATA ANALYSIS PEER REVIEW FORM

Name_____ **Date**_____

Are the data presented clearly?

Very clear	❏	Comments about what was done well:
Mostly clear	❏	
Somewhat clear	❏	Suggestions for improvement:
Largely unclear	❏	

Are the conclusions clearly stated?

Very clear	❏	Comments about what was done well:
Mostly clear	❏	
Somewhat clear	❏	Suggestions for improvement:
Largely unclear	❏	

Do the data clearly support the conclusions?

Very clear	❏	Comments about what was done well:
Mostly clear	❏	
Somewhat clear	❏	Suggestions for improvement:
Largely unclear	❏	

BEYOND PROTOCOLS:
CONDUCTING INTERACTIVE RESEARCH

IDEAS FOR BIOASSAY RESEARCH

Many types of experiments can be carried out using bioassays. The following discussion is designed to help you plan an interesting research project. We suggest that you start by filling out the ***Choosing a Research Topic*** worksheet (p. 90), and then read the sections below that cover topics you are interested in investigating.

DOSE/RESPONSE BIOASSAYS

After carrying out a dose/response experiment (Protocol 2, 3, or 4), you may have come up with further questions related to the response of the bioassay organisms to your test chemical.

For example, suppose that you carried out a lettuce seed bioassay using solutions at 100%, 10%, 1%, 0.1%, and 0.01% concentrations, and a distilled water control. None of the lettuce seeds sprouted at your 100% concentration, but all of the ones in the 10% concentration sprouted and grew as well as the control group. You might decide to carry out a new experiment using a series of solutions ranging between 10% and 100% concentrations.

Another possibility is that all the *Daphnia* exposed to your serial dilution died, or that none of the duckweed grew. In this case you might want to try even lower dilutions of the same chemical to see whether you can find a concentration in which the bioassay organisms will be able to survive and grow.

The following steps outline the general process involved in carrying out dose/response bioassay experiments:

1. First, decide what chemical you want to test. There are of course many possibilities. Think about chemicals that are used for various purposes in the environment, such as road salt or other ice-melting chemicals, or herbicides and pesticides commonly used on lawns, roadsides, and gardens.

2. Next, determine what concentrations to use in your bioassay. Before scientists begin an experiment, usually they search for scientific papers that relate to the procedure they have in mind. If you have access to scientific journals, a good way to get an idea about an appropriate range of concentrations would be to look for reports on bioassays using the organism and compound you have chosen. Another possibility is to read student reports posted on the EI website *http://ei.cornell.edu* to see if anyone has already generated data that would be useful to you.

3. If you can't find any appropriate data, that's OK—you'll just have to start with a broader range of concentrations to make sure you hit the range in which your test organism

responds. (With too high a concentration, the test organisms will all die, or in the case of seeds, none will sprout. With too low a concentration, you will not be able to detect any difference between your samples and your control.) Ideally, you want to test concentrations that cover both these endpoints plus a range of concentrations in between.

4. Once you have chosen a 100% concentration, then you can make a serial dilution according to Protocol 1 and carry out your bioassays according to Protocols 2, 3, and/or 4.

BIOASSAYS ON ENVIRONMENTAL SAMPLES

If you want to carry out bioassay experiments using environmental samples, a good way to start would be to think about places or circumstances where you would expect to find pollution. Then convert this into a question you could answer using bioassays.

Examples:

▶ Perhaps a student group is planning to hold a car wash in the school parking lot, and you are wondering whether the runoff will harm life in the creek into which the wash water will drain. You might ask: "What brand of detergent is least toxic to duckweed and *Daphnia*?"

▶ Another parking lot question might focus on the impacts of the motor oil and gas that sometimes drip from cars, and the dust and dirt that collect along the curbs. You might ask, "Does parking lot runoff contain chemicals that are toxic to lettuce seeds?" If this proves to be the case, you might go on to ask, "If we filtered out the dirt and other solids before storm runoff enters the creek, would the toxicity be reduced?"

▶ Other possible types of environmental samples that might be interesting to study include landfill leachate, runoff from golf courses or farms, and effluent from sewage treatment plants. Each of these is a complex mixture of many chemicals that may either enhance or impair the survival and growth of your bioassay organisms.

For example, sewage effluent probably contains nutrients that could trigger growth of bioassay organisms. However, it also is likely to contain chlorine, which might kill or injure the bioassay organisms. Chlorine is used to destroy germs before wastewater is released into the environment. If the effluent kills *Daphnia* in your bioassays, does this mean it will also kill the aquatic organisms in the lake or stream? To address this question, you would need to consider the dilution that occurs as the effluent mixes with water in the lake or stream. You could do a serial dilution of the effluent to determine at what dilution it becomes nontoxic to your bioassay organisms.

The results of your original experiment may lead you to further questions. For example, suppose that you carried out a bioassay using runoff from your school parking lot, and all of the *Daphnia* died except for those in the control group. You might want to follow up with experiments on questions such as the following:

▶ Is it possible, using ion exchange or activated charcoal treatment, to figure out what types of chemicals are causing the *Daphnia* to die?

▶ Does the toxicity of parking lot runoff change with the season, or perhaps with the amount of rainfall?

▶ Is runoff from other nearby parking lots also toxic to *Daphnia*?

▶ Are duckweeds and lettuce seeds also affected by parking lot runoff?

▶ At what percent dilution does car-wash detergent become nontoxic to each type of bioassay organism?

When interpreting your results, you should remember that bioassays test for toxicity, not for pollution. For example, runoff that is high in nutrients may make your bioassay organisms grow better than the control group. You might be tempted to conclude that this nutrient-rich runoff is good for the environment. However, suppose that this runoff water causes nuisance growth of aquatic plants in the pond or lake into which it drains. In this case, the runoff is not toxic but would still be considered a source of pollution.

DETOXIFICATION/CLASSIFICATION EXPERIMENTS

Detoxification experiments use ion exchange and/or activated charcoal treatment to remove toxic ions or compounds from two types of solution:

1. Solutions of known composition

2. Unknown mixtures of chemicals, such as environmental samples

In either case, follow-up bioassays will determine whether ion exchange or activated charcoal treatment has reduced the toxicity of the solution. This may help you to determine whether the chemical causing the toxicity was a cation, an anion, or a nonpolar molecule.

Solutions of Known Composition

In this type of experiment, you choose a chemical and then use ion exchange and/or activated charcoal columns to try to reduce the toxicity of the solution containing this compound. For example, suppose you ran an initial experiment and found that copper sulfate ($CuSO_4$) is toxic to *Daphnia*. You might decide to investigate whether this toxicity is caused by the Cu^{+2} cation or the SO_4^{-2} anion, or both. If you were to filter the copper sulfate solution through a cation exchange column, the copper ions would be removed from solution. Similarly, an anion exchange column would remove the sulfate ions. By using these treated filtrates for bioassay experiments, you should be able to compare the toxicity of the original solution and the solutions with each type of ion removed.

Unknown Mixtures of Chemicals

In this type of experiment, you start with an environmental sample such as drainage water from a ditch near your school. If the ditch water proves toxic to your bioassay organisms, there are many possible chemicals that could be causing this toxicity. Unlike the copper sulfate solution discussed above, the ditch water is made up of a complex mixture of many different chemicals. However, it still is possible to narrow down the types of compounds causing the toxicity by treating the sample using ion exchange and activated charcoal columns. If the effluent from one of these columns turns out to be nontoxic, then you will have identified whether the toxic substances are cations, anions, or uncharged compounds. On the other hand, perhaps there is more than one type of toxic compound in your mixture, so treatment with more than one type of column may be necessary for purification of environmental samples.

SC*L*INKS.
THE WORLD'S A CLICK AWAY

Topic: nutrient runoff
Go to: www.scilinks.org
Code: ATR11

Topic: water treatment
Go to: www.scilinks.org
Code: ATR07

OTHER POSSIBILITIES

Comparing Species

Within any one species, individuals respond differently when exposed to any particular chemical. You can observe this in *Daphnia* bioassays when some individuals die at low concentrations while others survive exposure to much higher doses. Between species, there are even greater differences in chemical sensitivities. For example, *Daphnia* may die at concentrations that do not seem to affect lettuce seeds or duckweed, or vice versa. For this reason, scientists rarely rely on a single type of bioassay organism. Commonly they choose at least one species of vertebrate, invertebrate, and plant, and then compare the sensitivities of these various types of organisms to the test compound or environmental samples.

With dose/response bioassays, you can compare the sensitivities of various species to a particular chemical by comparing the LC50 or TC50 values. Using Protocols 2–4, for example, you could expose two or three bioassay species to the same range of concentrations of your test compound and then compare sensitivities.

With environmental bioassays using samples such as the runoff from your school parking lot, again you can compare the LC50 or TC50 values to determine which species are most sensitive. The only difference here is that you won't know specifically what chemical or chemicals in the environmental samples are causing the toxicity to the test organisms.

Investigating Environmental Impacts

Bioassays provide a useful tool for investigating environmental issues related to chemical toxicity. For example, you might choose to look into the potential environmental impacts of the various chemicals that are used to melt ice on winter highways. Many towns in snowy parts of the country are trying to cut down on their use of road salt. Not only does the salt cause cars to rust, it also has environmental effects when the snow melts and salty water runs off into streams, rivers, and lakes.

One alternative is to use other chemical forms of salt. Normal road salt is sodium chloride (NaCl). Alternative deicing products that claim to be less corrosive and more environmentally friendly than road salt usually contain magnesium, calcium, or potassium chloride ($MgCl_2$, $CaCl_2$, or KCl).

There are many possibilities for experiments to assess the environmental effects of road salt or a deicing substitute. You could use one of the following questions, or create your own:

▶ Is $MgCl_2$, $CaCl_2$, or KCl less toxic to bioassay organisms than NaCl?

▶ By mixing these compounds, can you get the same or better melting power than NaCl, with less potential environmental impact?

▶ How much would you have to dilute the deicing product used on your school's sidewalks in order to make it nontoxic to bioassay organisms?

Before you begin, you could try calling your local highway department to ask what methods they use for highway deicing. Perhaps you can design an experiment to test the products being used in your community.

Road deicing is just one example of how you can use bioassays to investigate potential environmental impacts. Think of chemical use issues that are important in your community, and then see if you can come up with bioassay experiments that will help to address these issues.

Determining Optimal Conditions for Survival and Growth

When scientists design experiments, how do they decide what would make a good control? In the case of bioassays, it seems logical to expose the organisms in the control group to the same conditions as in the treatments, leaving out only the chemical that is being tested. The control would then consist of distilled or other relatively pure water rather than a test solution. Ideally, the control should promote optimal survival and growth so that any inhibition caused by toxic chemicals can be compared to what the growth would be under the best possible conditions. This provides the baseline against which the experimental treatments can be compared.

But what if your bioassay organisms survive or grow better in some of the treatments than in the control? Does this mean you've done something wrong? Not necessarily—it is quite possible that low concentrations of chemicals could enhance rather than inhibit growth of the test organisms. Think about experiments you could design to test optimal conditions for culturing lettuce seeds, duckweed, or *Daphnia*.

Lettuce Seeds

There are many experiments you could do to better define the optimal conditions for lettuce seed bioassays. For example, consider what experiments you might carry out to answer the following questions:

▶ What is the optimal pH for lettuce seed germination or radicle growth?

▶ What is the best amount of solution to use in each petri dish? (It varies in the scientific literature, with some investigators using less than 1 mL/dish and others using 5 or 10 mL/dish.)

▶ Is there a minimal salts solution that promotes better germination and growth rates than distilled water?

▶ What temperature is optimal?

These are important questions, and the answers to them are not currently available in scientific papers. The results of your experiments will add to what currently is known about the optimal conditions for lettuce seed germination and growth.

To determine what compounds might enhance lettuce seed germination and growth, and in what concentrations, a number of different experiments are possible. You might want to try adding a mineral compound that is commonly found in tap water, such as magnesium or calcium carbonate ($MgCO_3$ or $CaCO_3$). Another possibility would be to test the effects of supplying a nutrient such as ammonium nitrate (NH_4NO_3) or potassium phosphate (K_2HPO_4). See if you can come up with a recipe for a solution that promotes better lettuce seed growth than distilled water.

Duckweed

Although duckweed plants grow like a weed, entirely coating the surface of ponds and wetlands, they are not so easy to culture indoors. By addressing questions such as these, you can help define a protocol for optimal growth of duckweed under laboratory conditions:

▶ Is duckweed sensitive to the chlorine in tap water?

▶ How much fertilizer promotes optimal growth?

▶ Are there additional nutrients other than those in the fertilizer solution that would promote better duckweed growth?

▶ Under what lighting conditions does duckweed grow fastest?

▶ Is pH important?

Another interesting question is why duckweed can be found growing in even the most polluted ponds and ditches, in spite of the fact that it is sensitive to some common pollutants. How can this be? One possible explanation is that because duckweed grows and reproduces so quickly, its populations can evolve and adapt to living in polluted environments. You could test this idea by comparing the sensitivities of duckweed plants from various sources. For example, you could test whether duckweed populations found in highway ditches show decreased sensitivity to pollutants such as oil or salt compared with duckweed from a pond that does not receive highway runoff.

Daphnia

Sometimes when *Daphnia* are delivered in the mail from a scientific supply company, most of the organisms are dead on arrival, and sometimes a culture that has been growing for months in a laboratory suddenly fails and all the organisms die. One possible set of experiments would be to look for reasons why a population might suddenly crash—what are the critical factors for keeping a culture alive?

A related study would be to investigate factors that are important over the long term for keeping a culture healthy and nonstressed. In a good environment, most *Daphnia* are female and will reproduce without breeding. When reproducing this way, the eggs do not get fertilized, so the young are exact copies of their mothers. The unfertilized eggs develop into live embryos inside the female's body, and the young are released into the environment within two to three days (see Figure 3.5).

When the environment becomes stressful, *Daphnia* adapt by producing male as well as female embryos. Once these individuals become mature, they breed and produce fertilized eggs that are encased in tough protective shells. These resting eggs are released from the female's body and will have to go through several cycles of freezing and thawing before they hatch.

Why do *Daphnia* respond to stress by reproducing sexually? This produces young that are not exact copies of their mothers, and some of the babies may be genetically more fit than others to cope with the stressful environment in which they must live. In addition, the fertilized eggs are enclosed in tough shells that help to protect them until the environment once again becomes favorable. This is a useful evolutionary adaptation for organisms that live in ponds or other water bodies that may dry up for part of the year—although the adults will die, their eggs are adapted to surviving until the environment once again becomes favorable.

If you are interested in experimenting with culture conditions necessary to maintain a nonstressed population of *Daphnia*, you could begin by considering factors that are likely to be important, such as population density, amount of food, temperature, pH, and dissolved

FIGURE 3.5
Identification Sheet for *Daphnia*

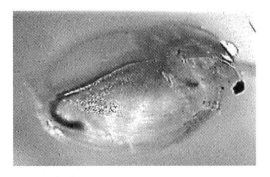

Female with empty brood chamber.

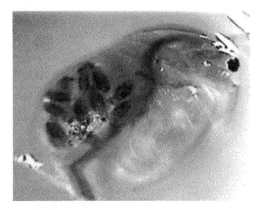

Female with asexual (unfertilized) eggs that will develop into live embryos before being released from the mother's body. Using a microscope, you may be able to see the embryos wiggling inside the mother's body.

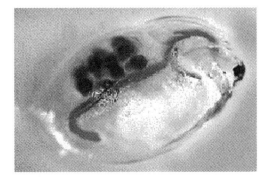

Female with sexual resting eggs encased in tough shells. These will be released from the female and will hatch when environmental conditions become favorable.

oxygen concentration. Then you could design experiments based on one or more of these factors. Be sure to change only one condition for each treatment, and use several replicates of each.

To determine which populations are stressed, you can examine adult *Daphnia* under a microscope to see whether the females' brood chambers contain live embryos rather than resting eggs, or you can simply watch your cultures over a period of several weeks. If at the end of this time you have a thriving population that is still producing young, you can conclude that you have provided nonstressful conditions. If the population dies out, either suddenly or gradually, obviously some factor was not suitable for *Daphnia* survival. Based on the results of your experiments, what conditions seem to be most critical?

WORKSHEETS FOR INTERACTIVE RESEARCH

See Table 4, p. 11 in the *Teacher's Guide* for a description of where each of these forms fits in the Environmental Inquiry (EI) research process.

CHOOSING A RESEARCH TOPIC

Name _____ **Date** _____

Would the organisms do better at lower concentrations of the same chemical?

What would happen at higher concentrations?

What other chemicals might provide an interesting comparison?

Can the solutions be cleaned up to make them less toxic?

Would other species react the same way?

What other kinds of samples would be interesting to test?

1. Make a list here of questions that you would be interested in investigating using bioassay experiments. Try to ask questions that are relevant to environmental issues.

   Example: *Does chlorinated tap water kill* Daphnia?

2. Of these questions, which seem the most important and interesting? Pick three:

1.

2.

3.

3. For each of the three questions you have chosen, think of how you might design an experiment. Then fill out this form:

Potential Questions

Question	Brief description of an experiment you might do to address this question	What equipment and supplies would you need?	How long would it take to carry out this project?	Would fieldwork or travel to field sites be required?
Example: Do Daphnia *die in chlorinated tap water?*	*Place* Daphnia *in tap water samples from school and from home.*	*Beakers, tap water samples,* Daphnia	*One period to set up beakers with* Daphnia, *a few minutes the next two days to count how many have died.*	*We can collect tap water at home and bring it in to school.*
Question 1:				
Question 2:				
Question 3:				

4. Looking over your questions, consider whether each project would be feasible for you to carry out. Are the equipment and supplies available? Do you have enough time? Will you be able to do whatever fieldwork is needed? Eliminate any questions that do not seem feasible based on logistics such as these.

	Would this project be feasible?	Why or why not?
Example Project	<u>Yes</u> No	*Uses supplies we have available + tap water we will bring in from home.*
Project 1	Yes No	
Project 2	Yes No	
Project 3	Yes No	

5. Choose a project you have decided is feasible and interesting and then continue on to the *Interactive Research Planning Sheet #1 or #2.*

INTERACTIVE RESEARCH PLANNING SHEET #1
(for exploratory level experiments)

Name _____ Date_____

1. **What question have you chosen to investigate, and why?**

    Example: Do Daphnia *die in chlorinated tap water? This question is important because it will help us to figure out whether we need to buy bottled spring water to keep our* Daphnia *alive.*

2. **Briefly describe a project you would like to do to address this question:**

    Example: We plan to place Daphnia *in tap water we collect from home and school. We will count how many have died after one day and two days.*

3. **What supplies will you need? How will you get any that are not already available in our classroom?**

    Example: Six beakers, tap water samples, Daphnia. *We will bring in tap water samples from home, and everything else is already here.*

4. **How do you plan to schedule your project?**

   Example: Monday— bring in tap water, measure it into beakers, add Daphnia.
   Tuesday—Count how many Daphnia *have died.*
   Wednesday—Count how many Daphnia *have died.*

5. **Can you find reports by other students or professional scientists on this topic? If so, what can you learn from what has already been done?**

6. **Meet with another student or group to discuss these plans using the *Experimental Design Peer Review Form*. Then describe any changes you've decided to make based on this discussion.**

INTERACTIVE RESEARCH PLANNING SHEET #2
(for rigorously designed experiments)

Name _____   Date _____

1. What question do you plan to investigate?

Example: At what concentration is copper sulfate toxic to Daphnia?

2. Why is this question important or relevant to environmental issues?

Example: Copper sulfate is used to kill algae in ponds but may also be toxic to other aquatic organisms.

3. Can you find reports by other students or professional scientists on this topic? If so, what can you learn from what has already been done?

4. What is your hypothesis (the prediction of what you think will happen, stated in a way that can be tested by doing an experiment)? Why did you choose this prediction?

Example: The concentration of copper sulfate used to kill algae in ponds will also be toxic to Daphnia. *This is my prediction because I have seen some dead fish in my grandparents' pond after they treated it with copper sulfate.*

5. **What is your independent variable** (the factor that you will change to make one treatment different from another)?

    Example: The independent variable in a dose/response experiment is the concentration of the test chemical.

6. **What is your dependent variable?** (This is the factor you will measure to determine the results of the experiment—it is called "dependent" because the results depend on changes in the independent variable from one treatment to the next.)

    Example: The dependent variable in a dose/response experiment could be the number of organisms that survive or the amount of growth that occurs.

    > If you are confused about the independent and dependent variables, it may help to think back to your research question and then think about how you might want to present the results of your experiment. For example, for a bioassay using *Daphnia*, you might set up a graph that looks something like the one below before you've entered the data.
    >
    > On the x-axis is your independent variable. These are the numbers that you decide in advance, to create your various treatments. For dose/response experiments, the most common independent variable is the series of concentrations of your test solution.
    >
    > On the y-axis is your dependent variable. This is the factor you will be measuring in your experiment, such as the length of the lettuce roots or the number of *Daphnia* that die at each concentration.

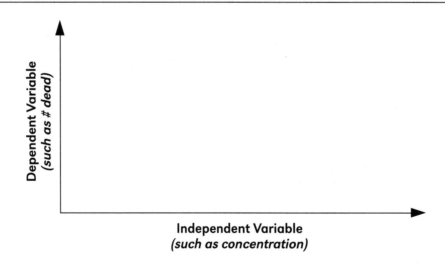

Independent Variable
(such as concentration)

7. What **treatments** do you plan? (Each level of your independent variable is a treatment. You should plan to change only the independent variable from one treatment to the next, keeping all other conditions constant.)

Example: What chemical concentrations will you test, or where will your environmental samples come from?

8. How many **replicates** will you have for each treatment? (These are groups of organisms that are exposed to exactly the same conditions.)

Example: Each beaker containing Daphnia is one replicate for that particular concentration of the test solution. In a lettuce seed bioassay, each petri dish containing seeds and test solution is one replicate. The more replicates you can manage, the better, but you will have to figure out how many are possible with the supplies and time you have available.

9. What is your **control** (the untreated group that serves as a standard of comparison)?

Example: In bioassays, organisms in the control group are grown in distilled or spring water rather than a chemical solution or an environmental sample. The organisms in the control group should be exposed to all the same conditions as the organisms in the treatment groups, except for the one variable you are testing, such as concentration.

10. What factors will you keep **constant** for all treatments? (The constants in an experiment are all the factors that do not change.)

Examples: temperature or light.

11. What equipment and supplies will you need?

12. What schedule will you follow? Think about how many days will be needed for growth of your bioassay organisms.

13. What will you measure and how will you display your data? Sketch an empty data table here, with the appropriate headings. Think about what kind of table you will need to record the data from your experiment.

On this graph, add labels for the x axis and y axis and sketch your expected results.

A Final Check: Evaluate Your Experimental Design

1. Does your planned experiment actually test your *hypothesis*?

2. Are you changing only one *variable* at a time? Which one?

3. Will your *control* be exposed to exactly the same conditions as your *treatments* (except for the *independent variable*)?

4. How many *replicates* will you have for each *treatment*?

5. Meet with another student or group to discuss these plans using the ***Experimental Design Peer Review Form***. Then describe any changes you've decided to make based on this discussion.

BIOASSAY RESEARCH REPORT FORM

Name _____ Date _____

1. What is the title of your research project?

2. What is your research question? Why is this question significant to environmental or other real-world issues?

3. What type of bioassay organisms did you use?

4. What substance(s) did you test?

5. Summarize your procedures here.

6. Summarize your data here.

   (Use the first row to label the columns. It's OK to leave rows and columns blank—just use the ones you need.)

Concentration or Type of Sample	Effect (such as germination rate)	Effect (such as radicle length)

7. Graph and then summarize your data. What is your interpretation of the meaning of these results?

8. What conclusions can you reach? (What did you learn from your experiment? Can you think of any other possible explanations for your results?)

9. If you were to repeat the experiment, what would you change in order to learn more about the toxicity of the substance(s) you studied? (Did you come up with any questions you couldn't answer using your data? Can you think of experiments that would help to answer these questions?)

10. What might you change to improve your experimental design?

POSTER DESIGN GUIDELINES

Posters are one way in which scientists present their research results. When posters are displayed at conferences, researchers have the opportunity to discuss their findings and ideas with fellow scientists.

At a poster session, people tend to spend the most time looking at posters that are attractive, well organized, and easy to read. It's best to keep the text short and to illustrate your points with graphs, photos, and diagrams.

To make your poster effective, make sure that it is:

Readable—Can your text be read from 2 meters away? (20 points is a good font size.)

Understandable—Do your ideas fit together and make sense?

Organized—Is your work summarized clearly, using the headings listed in the example below?

Attractive—Will your poster make viewers want to take the time to read it? Have you used illustrations and color to enhance your display, without making the text hard to read?

Here is an example poster layout:

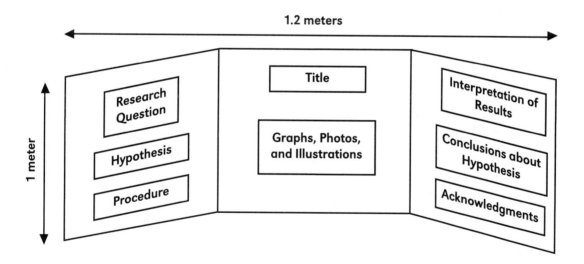

EXPERIMENTAL DESIGN PEER REVIEW FORM

Name of Reviewer _____ Date _____

Project Reviewed _____

Is the research question clearly defined?

Very clear	❏	**Comments about what was done well:**
Mostly clear	❏	
Somewhat clear	❏	**Suggestions for improvement:**
Largely unclear	❏	

Are the procedures clearly described?

Very clear	❏	**Comments about what was done well:**
Mostly clear	❏	
Somewhat clear	❏	**Suggestions for improvement:**
Largely unclear	❏	

How well does this experiment address the research question?

Very clear	❏	**Comments about what was done well:**
Mostly clear	❏	
Somewhat clear	❏	**Suggestions for improvement:**
Largely unclear	❏	

RESEARCH REPORT PEER REVIEW FORM

Name of Reviewer_____   Date_____

Project Reviewed   _____

After reading a Bioassay Research Report written by other students, answer the following questions. Remember to keep your answers friendly and constructive.

1. What was a particular strength in this experimental design?

2. Do you agree with the conclusions? Do they appear to be supported by the results of the experiment?

3. What suggestions can you make for improving this experiment or report?

POSTER PEER REVIEW FORM

Name of Reviewer_____ Date_____

Project Reviewed _____

KEY
1—Largely unclear
2—Somewhat clear
3—Mostly clear
4—Very clear

	(-)		(+)
Does the poster include: Title, Research Question, Hypothesis, Procedure, Results, Conclusions, and Acknowledgments?	1 2 3 4
Is there a clear statement of the research question and hypothesis?	1 2 3 4
Does the experiment appear to be designed appropriately to address the research question?	1 2 3 4
Are the procedures described in enough detail for the experiment to be copied by someone else?	1 2 3 4
Are the data presented clearly?	1 2 3 4
Is there a clear explanation of the results?	1 2 3 4
Do the conclusions seem well supported by the data?	1 2 3 4
Were the presenters able to answer questions clearly?	1 2 3 4
Is the poster attractive and easy to read and understand?	1 2 3 4

TOTAL SCORE _____

COMMENTS:
What was a particular strength of this experimental design?

What suggestions do you have for improving either this experiment or the poster presentation?